To the ancestors and saints who formed my understanding of Jesus Christ through their unapologetic activism, spiritual care, acts of kindness, and liberating creativity.

PROPHETS,
PRIESTS,
PASTORS,
& POETS

PROPHETS, PRIESTS, PASTORS, & POETS

Being and Becoming the Resurrected Christ

BRUCE REYES-CHOW

chalice
PRESS

Print: 9780827231948

EPUB: 9780827231955

EPDF: 9780827231962

ChalicePress.com

Printed in the United States of America

Contents

Preface

Dear reader,

It is crucial for you, dear reader, to know the particular time and context in which I am writing about Jesus. This book was written in 2025 into 2026, and unprecedented does not come close to describing what we are going through as a country and culture.

In all honesty, this has been a difficult book to write, not because I do not care about Jesus—I do (good thing as a pastor)—but because it is difficult to hole away, sit down, and focus on what feels like a detached and futile endeavor while our country's socioeconomic and political chasms are widening, countless people are subjected to government-sponsored terror, and people of faith and privilege like me are being called to the street. I wish this was just another example of drama and hyperbole, but at the completion of this book, about a year into the second presidential term of Donald Trump, the number of truly horrifying events that have taken place over that time would be comical if those events were not so tragic.

- At the time of publication, we are "celebrating" the 250th birthday of the United States, and in the same week the Supreme Court has gutted the Voting Rights Act of 1965.
- We are experiencing the ramifications of our government choosing to enter into an act of war against Iran, further destabilizing the region and testing relationships with global partners.
- Thirty or more people have died in Immigration and Customs Enforcement (ICE) incidents, and three people have been shot and killed by ICE agents: Keith Porter Jr., Reneé Nicole Good, and Alex Pretti.
- Because of protesting over the genocide in Gaza and the United States' support of the nation of Isreal, university students and faculty have been arrested, suspended, expelled, and fired.

The United States has severely cut back or eliminated international support by closing down USAID and withdrawing from multiple international organizations and agreements such as the Paris Climate Accords, the World Health Organization, and dozens of other humanitarian and international support agencies. The United States has executed a military action against Venezuela, which included capturing the president and his wife under the pretenses of "national security," "America First," "drug war," and getting back oil that was "stolen from us."

- The United States government had the longest shutdown in its history and continues to engage in partisan gamesmanship while many believe we have drifted into a state of authoritarianism.
- The president has deployed the National Guard and federalized other agencies to police US citizens in multiple cities during protests of immigration activities. Anyone suspected of being an undocumented immigrant is at risk of being kidnapped off the streets by masked ICE agents and deported to prisons around the world.
- People are losing jobs for protesting just about anything.
- Measles are making a comeback, vaccine protocols are being rolled back decades, and vaccines and acetaminophen are being blamed for autism.
- The United States is bombing ships in international waters in the name of a war on drug trafficking.
- Gun violence continues to plague our culture.
- The United States has decided to opt out of all global and national efforts to curb climate change by leaving the Paris Climate Accords and dismantling all green and renewable energy efforts in the United States.
- Public xenophobic, racist, misogynistic, and queerphobic rhetoric is platformed at the highest levels like never before in my lifetime.

The wealth gap is growing, health insurance is unaffordable, education costs are skyrocketing, homophobia is being legislated,

Islamophobia is being ignored, birthright citizenship is being challenged, antisemitism is on the rise, reproductive rights are being stripped, and in just about every other area of society where marginalized and vulnerable people exist, our government is finding a way to insert its brand of cruelty and terror into their lives.

Again, I wish this were hyperbolic, but it is not.

In fact, I sincerely believe this cruelty is by design, and not in the name of ideology or theology, but to build and maintain global power and material wealth by any means. Sadly, conservative Evangelical Christianity and Christian nationalism are among the vehicles used to carry and reinforce these messages.

This is the particular context in which I write these words: The United States is experiencing a rise of Christian nationalism and old-school puritanism dressed up in twenty-first-century politics. Books are banned for being too sexual, we are overly concerned with other people's genitalia, same-gender marriage is under attack, trans folks are being used as political pawns, and yet the "Christians are being persecuted" trope is wheeled out at every turn. Sadly, right-wing conservative activist Charlie Kirk was assassinated, and his funeral was a flash point for Christian nationalism, an amalgamation of political rally, pre-battle frenzy, and Christian worship. This was capped off when Secretary of Defense Pete Hegseth published a video of himself leading the Lord's Prayer during a memorial for Kirk on a US aircraft carrier, overlaid with a montage of military and warfare images. No longer is Christian nationalism hiding in the shadows; it is being flaunted at the highest levels of our government.

God and the Bible have been weaponized, Christianity is being corrupted beyond recognition, and it seems as though our slow drift into theocracy and ideological apartheid has gone into a nitro-powered frenzy because, as a whole, there has not been enough political will to stop them.

That does not mean that no one is trying. Thankfully, many are stepping up.

Public actions are happening throughout the country; friends and colleagues are using the power of the pulpit to invite their communities to the struggles; folks are organizing their communities; and many are putting themselves at risk on behalf of those who cannot. So while I sometimes want to crawl into my warm, comfy bed of privilege and wait until this is all over, I know that God has different plans for me and so many others. I am inspired by those prophets, priests, pastors, and poets of the past, the present, and those yet to come who remind me that in a day when violent and insidious powers want us to succumb to terror, repression, and despair, it is vital to reaffirm with bold abandon that freedom, hope, and love will always win the day.

It is with that inspiration, and with 2025 in the rearview mirror and 2026 before me, that I complete this particular project. While every author hopes their work will age well over time, I hope this offering will soon seem outrageously hyperbolic in nature, because it will mean that the context will have changed for the better. I fear, however, that what has been breached will take generations to repair. So until that time, on this day, and in the face of the evil acts we witness, I humbly but boldly offer and invite you to consider a different way of embracing the gospel and to move through this time in the activist, disciplined, empathetic, and imaginative ways of Jesus.

I hope you will join me on this journey of faithful exploration; we all learn more when we endeavor together.

Trusting in the Resurrection,

Bruce

Introduction

Who do people say that I am? —Mark 6:27

We begin this particular Jesus journey with a screaming toddler on a cold Christmas Eve night. It was the late '90s, and we had been trucking it from the Christmas Eve service that I led as the pastor of a local congregation to our family gathering. Every year, the rest of the family had to wait for my mom (also a Presbyterian minister) and me to finish our services before the feasting could begin. We were all getting a little tired and cranky. During this particular service, Jesus stickers were handed out to the kids as a way for them to remember that Jesus is with them, with us, and with the world. When we left service, Jesus was firmly in Ev's hand, but by the time we arrived, Ev had fallen asleep and released their grip, allowing Jesus to disappear into the wilderness of a minivan abyss of goldfish crackers, single socks, and mysterious substances. When we pulled up to the driveway of my mom's place and Ev woke up, we were greeted with the type of scream that only comes from an abruptly awakened hungry toddler.

"I lost Jesus!" was all we heard over and over and over again. "I lost Jesus! I lost Jesus! I lost Jesus!"

Being the loving, straitlaced, pious church parents that we were, we could only giggle to ourselves as we tried to comfort our child, who was so clearly distressed about losing Jesus. Seriously, we could barely hold in our outright laughter while trying to console our screaming child. And, miracles of miracles, Jesus somehow showed up, and Ev triumphantly declared, "I found him. I found Jesus!"

Whew. Crisis of faith averted.

This is where we begin with Jesus. Make no mistake, I take Jesus very seriously. And at the same time, I do not take us humans too seriously in our pursuit of understanding this divine human we call the

Christ. We are complex people deserving of all the reactions when it comes to how we have approached Jesus: compassion, encouragement, gratitude, patience, and yes, even sometimes a little playful mockery.

Now, you might be saying to yourself, "Um, what the hell? People trust this guy with their spiritual well-being? I have definitely been duped!" So let me be even clearer about what you have gotten yourself into by picking up this book. What you are about to enter (I say that like this is some amusement park haunted house disclaimer) is not going to be a densely academic or highfalutin theological treatise about Jesus. The pages that follow are an invitation, prompting, and encouragement to explore the Jesus you probably have always known and to dive a little deeper. I intend for this book to provide you with a way to stretch and strengthen what you have had inklings about but may have been too embarrassed, unsure, or ashamed to ask out loud. I want to tease out the wisdom, curiosities, and wonderings from within because when we do that collectively, I truly believe that the Jesus we all know becomes more alive for us all.

Who Is This For?

So who is this book for? Well, it is not meant to be casually dropped in front of that unsuspecting person at the café so you can loudly proclaim, "Ooops, I just dropped my copy of my book about Jesus. Would you mind picking it up for me?" I say this because this book is not meant to prove why one should believe in Jesus Christ. If this is your hope, you will be disappointed. The intention of *Prophets, Priests, Pastors, & Poets* is to offer one more lens through which folks may view the nature of Jesus in the world, should they be curious about or considering Jesus, both individually and communally. As one who has chosen Christianity as my faith home, I would not mind if others choose the same path; but to be clear from the get-go, I will not say that Jesus is the *only* way to experience the Divine.

What I hope to offer is a textured understanding of Jesus that may meet folks in various stages of curiosity, confusion, and contemplation:

- If you are curious about Jesus for the first or fiftieth time, I hope the Jesus I offer is a meaningful one. If you have had Jesusadjacent experiences through friends or family and are now interested in diving a little deeper, I hope you will be inspired to keep exploring on your own or with others.

- If you have been frustrated by the domesticated version of Jesus, one marked by indifference about the injustices of the world, I hope to share Jesus, the disrupter and teller of truth.
- If you are tired of the one-dimensional version of Jesus that is expressed only in words, only in actions, or only personally, I hope to share Jesus, the holder of the richness of discipline and tradition.
- If you have been harmed or traumatized by the ways Jesus has been weaponized against you and others, I hope to share Jesus, the gatherer, healer, and cultivator of belonging.
- If you are drained by the version of Jesus that lacks inspiration, imagination, and joy, I hope to share Jesus, the creative unleasher of imagination.

After nearly thirty years of ministry, I am still on the same journey as so many others in understanding and following Jesus, meaning that my faith is always in flux. My personal and communal understanding and experiences with Jesus shift, change, and adapt as the world's circumstances dictate. While some see a change in theological understanding as a weakness, I see it as a strength. Just as my actual muscles need to be stretched and strengthened as my physical body moves through different stages of life, my spiritual and theological muscles must do the same when my experience of the world expands. I am constantly amazed by the revelations about my faith that abound when I embrace the idea that I will never be done getting to know the one we call Jesus the Christ. In short, this book is as much about my own exploration and learning as it is about yours. So welcome and thank you for taking me along.

Why Another Book about Jesus?

In 2024, I wrote a book titled *Everything Good about God Is True: Choosing Faith,* which was a sweeping primer on Christianity. Yes, the whole thing. While I will borrow a few nuggets from that book in *Prophets, Priests, Pastors, & Poets*, I will focus solely on Jesus. I am doing this because I have found that too often when people describe and define Jesus, they pigeonhole him into whatever theological, cultural, or political box reinforces their theological, cultural, or political beliefs. For many, Jesus has been weaponized as the armed gatekeeping secret agent to God. For others, Jesus is the lowly and gentle tree hugger on some random beach in the tropics. And yet for others, Jesus is a badass radical prophet turning over tables and pissing people off at every turn. And while there are some aspects of falsities and truths in each depiction, I have found none of them helpful in and of themselves.

What I love most about the faith I grew up with is that it has offered me unique and complex truths in the person of Jesus Christ. Note I say "truths" and not "the" truth, for whether one has claimed Christian faith for a lifetime or is exploring it for the first time, we must all continually ask ourselves: Why? Why believe? What does it mean for our daily lives? And what does it mean for how we make a difference in the world, especially in a world that is in constant and tumultuous flux culturally, politically, and ideologically? The specificity of truth shifts and changes as we learn and grow over time. Some may see this as relativism and a lack of conviction, while I see this as an ability to grow, adapt, and listen to the Spirit. Truths about God's hope, peace, joy, and love certainly do not change, but exactly how those truths manifest themselves in our lives and in the world certainly does.

With this in mind, we must continue exploring and give ourselves permission to shift, change, and grow. Thankfully, there is no linear path toward understanding most ideas, let alone Jesus. Yes, it may be tempting to believe that there is a fixed number of definitive, unchanging truths about Jesus. *Jesus said "X," so that means "X" now and forevermore even if we learn something new about the world, the speaker, or the hearer* is not a faithful way to understand Jesus' guidance for our lives. Not only would that be a boring way to live, but it would also deprive us of the depth and texture that are so beautifully woven through Jesus' ever-shifting, ever-evolving, and ever-expanding relationship with humanity.

So if you are game for a bit of beautiful and chaotic wandering and revelatory wondering about the person of Jesus Christ, again, welcome.

Who Do We Say Jesus Is?

It would be tempting to write a book about Jesus and only lift up the versions of him that I think are true and ignore the reality that there are narratives about Jesus being peddled that I wholeheartedly renounce. While I will not center this book around who Jesus is not, it is important for me to name some of the ways that Jesus shows up in culture and politics to remain aware and empathetic to the fact that this book does not and will not exist in a vacuum. The dangerous and destructive stories of Jesus that have been whispered and shouted in the ears of so many must be named. I start here with a list of versions of Jesus that I believe must be challenged. In no particular order, these are the stories of Jesus I reject:

> *The Punisher Jesus:* The Jesus who will kick your ass if you do the wrong thing. And yes, that list of what is right or wrong is *completely* objective. (That's sarcasm, just to be clear.)
>
> *The Warrior Jesus:* The Jesus who is "locked and loaded" and given some kind of lethality as manifested in physical appearance, weaponry, violence, etc., aka...
>
> *The Superhero Jesus:* The ripped, costumed Jesus who will swoop down from the sky and rescue us just as we are about to be crushed by our enemies.
>
> *The Santa Claus Jesus:* The Jesus who will give us all the things we ask for as long as we stay on the right side of that ledger. Again, that list is *completely* objective (still sarcasm).
>
> *The Misquoted Jesus:* The Jesus who said, "Pull yourself up by your bootstraps," "God helps those who help themselves," "I definitely care who wins at the sportsball game!" or "Homosexuality is a sin."
>
> *The Partisan Jesus:* Nope, there may be parts of what the [insert any political party here] stands for that align with

Jesus' teachings, but way too many humans are influenced by power, wealth, and the maintenance of institutions or empire for Jesus to be a registered member of *any* party—elephant, donkey, tree, or sickle.

The Nice Jesus: Jesus as the one who never makes waves and just wants everyone to get along. The Jesus I follow was kind and empathetic—never cruel or dehumanizing. (Okay, maybe once with the Syrophoenician woman, but he realized his mistake.) Remember, he was crucified for challenging empire and authority, so he was definitely not "nice."

The Blond, Blue-eyed, All-American Jesus: I am all for contextualizing Jesus in order to help us understand who he is to a community. But when those interpretations are weaponized and construed as facts, we get results like Christian nationalism fueled by white supremacy.

A quick word about other traditions in relation to Jesus. No surprise, but I am not much interested in putting Jesus into a divinity contest with other religious traditions. To try to prove one faith tradition over the other is a fool's errand, a poor use of time, and a recipe for broken relationships, spiritual trauma, and physical violence. I believe that God has spoken, speaks now, and will continue to speak to humanity in a variety of ways. I have simply chosen to believe that it is through Jesus Christ that I gain access to a relationship with God now and forever. This is a personal choice of faith and not one that I assume is or should be for everyone. I do not spend energy or time trying to convince others that they are right or wrong. My time is better spent modeling a life lived in response to the faith of my choosing, Christianity; and if people respond to that, great! If they inquire and seek to know what Christianity is about, also great; if not, fine too. I am under no delusions that our way is the only way humanity has to understand its relationship with the Divine.

And finally, if it is not already abundantly clear, I believe that Jesus is inherently political (but we must not cheapen his message by confining him to that "Partisan Jesus" described above). No matter what lens through which you approach the world, all values and viewpoints impact the communities and systems within which we live. As we all are, Jesus, too, was part of the body politic, navigating the maze of politics, power, and personalities of the day. The body politic is analogous to the body of Christ. As such, and as we know from 1 Corinthians 12:26–27, "If one part suffers, all the parts suffer with it; if one part gets the glory, all the parts celebrate with it. You are the body of Christ and parts of each other." This is what it means to be political, to bring healing where there is hurt so that the entire body may rejoice. Tending to the body politic is politics at its best, and I see the teachings of Jesus as deeply political.

Who Is Telling Us Who Jesus Is?

An essential element of who we say Jesus is is who has told us who Jesus is. Just as our individual identities are not formed in a vacuum, neither are our understandings of Jesus, be they positive, negative, or in between. Just as recognizing the influences (family origin, culture, trauma, etc.) that have formed us can help us grow as individuals and in relationship with others, doing the same can help us grow in our understanding and relationship with Jesus.

When I mentioned all the tropes about Jesus (hero, Santa, warrior, American, etc.), what did you picture Jesus looking like? What was he doing? What images were missing? Was there discomfort between what you pictured and who you have known Jesus to be in your actual experience? Where did you get your images of Jesus?

I do not think any of us can say that our understanding of Jesus comes from one single source. We are all influenced by culture, media, and social norms. And when it comes to faith, we are even more impacted by those close to us: family, friends, and community. Our ancestors and saints, society and culture, our own imaginations and experiences, scriptural interpretations, and theological and faith traditions have communicated our vision of who Jesus is. I wish I could say that these are always positive influences, but we all know this is not the case. A justified critique and rejection of the Christian faith is the historic destruction that has been done in the name of Jesus. It would be foolish to deny this. So many influences in the world have done irreparable harm to communities by reinforcing images of Jesus that run counter to those I will offer in this book. Many of you may already hold these harmful ideas. And yet I will suggest that we keep the dangerous images and understandings of Jesus alongside the ones that are liberating. It is important to hold both in tension as you venture through this book and interact with the images that I offer so you can continue to discern and discover who Jesus is for you now, be in conversation with who Jesus has been for you in the past, and yes, prepare yourself to be open to discover who Jesus may be for you in the future.

Who Would Jesus Say We Are?

So this is where the "being and becoming" come in. For my entire ministry, I have always been a "So what?" pastor. We can talk about faith, we can talk about Jesus, we can talk about the church, but "So what?" What does it mean to the world and our actions in it? And specifically, what does it mean for us to believe in this ridiculous and outrageous claim of the resurrection of Jesus Christ and our inclusion as part of the body of Christ?

So here is the "So what?"

We are invited to be and become God's greatest hopes and intentions for humanity as witnessed through the life, death, and resurrection of Jesus Christ.

The simplicity of what may feel like a complicated calling is modeled in Christ himself. Jesus is fully human and fully divine, striving to be and become, seeing the present and the possible, seeing the difficulties of the day and still believing in a hope for tomorrow. Too often with the weight of the present, we get bogged down by the belief that all there is the "now." We have lost the capacity to imagine a new, better world, essentially neutering the Jesus within. I challenge us to imitate Jesus when we feel stuck. We must not ignore the struggles and hardships of the world, and we must be receptive to the teaching of Jesus who models for us disruptive, disciplined, relational, and imaginative ways to move from who we are to who we can become over and over again: Jesus the Prophet, Priest, Pastor, and Poet.

How to Use This Book

As I mentioned earlier, throughout my entire ministry and in my writings, when exploring all aspects of faith, I have always asked myself the question "So what?" All the prayers, preaching, and potlucks are meaningless unless these actions help us to be the church that we believe God intends for us to be in the world: prophetic, priestly, pastoral, and poetic.

- Every time I have preached about injustice—"So what? What does this mean about how we will act to bring about justice?"
- Every time I have preached about spiritual disciples—"So what? How will this inform and ground our actions in the world so they align with what we have discerned are God's intentions?"
- Every time I have preached about empathy—"So what? How will this center the lives of those struggling in body, mind, and spirit to tend to spaces of healing and wholeness?"
- Every time I have preached about possibility, "So what? How will our expansive understanding of God bring about a world of unimaginable hope, peace, joy, and love?"

I am under no delusions that I have been successful in all instances. But in this book about Jesus, I will unapologetically and obnoxiously attempt to answer these very questions, challenge us to stay focused on the breadth and depth of Christ, and not be distracted by the elements that only we face. To be clear, this is not about answering those questions with tidy and trite answers or productivity goals; rather, it's a challenge to have Jesus' life, death, and resurrection actually mean something in *all aspects* of our lives and, God willing, in the lives of others.

Whoa, *all* aspects? Yes, you read that right. I am a firm believer that there are very few neutral situations or interactions in life, so the more integrated we can become with Jesus' calling in our individual and communal lives, the better we all move through the world together. No, God is not some creeper peering into all moments of our private and public lives, but how we conduct ourselves and build relationships with those near or far is fueled by an understanding that the Spirit of God is somehow at work.

Again, this book will not get you to the point that you can stand toe-to-toe with any Jesus scholar or anyone who makes the memorization of scripture into an art form. This book serves as a jumping-off point and an unapologetic instigator of conversation rather than a definitive and status explanation of who Jesus is for any one of us. This is not a cop-out; it is an exercise in claiming that the more we explore and stretch our individual and communal understanding of Jesus, the more interwoven he becomes in our everyday lives. Yes, some see certainty as the ultimate fruit of faith, while I will state boldly that curiosity, exploration, and openness are the ultimate cultivators of faith.

At the beginning of each of the four sections I have compiled, with the help of friends on the interwebs, a list of "You might be a ____ if..." statements appear as a way to playfully spark something in you.

Within each chapter, I offer some background about each area, how Jesus manifests in each area, how we may do so, and then ten prompts for how you or your community may do the same. At the end of each chapter, I will pose a few questions for you and for any group that may be reading this together. And then at the end of each chapter, I offer a litany for communal usage for a small group or worship service.

The big "So what?" of this book will be that you will be able to boldly and unapologetically answer the question, "How does embracing the fourfold nature of Christ impact how I/we will participate in bringing about the possibilities that Christ offers to the world?"

A Word about the Bible

Throughout the book, I will lean heavily on the Bible to provide examples of Jesus healing, challenging, caring, questioning, comforting, and generally living his life. You need not be a biblical scholar to understand these. I hope to give enough context that you get the point and maybe are spurred on to read more.

I always attempt to read and absorb the Bible with a nuanced spirit, and I invite you to do the same. I believe the Bible tells the breadth and depth of the human experience with God. It both liberates and binds and is a living conversation and delicate dance between humanity and the Spirit. The Bible contains a record of God's story as told by authors who sought to discern God's movement in the story of their people. More specifically, the Bible operates as a living guidebook for our lives. The Bible guides us into understanding God's faithfulness to us. While some see scripture as clear and concise rules for life, I don't. In fact, the Bible is anything but clear or concise. But I do believe that reading scripture challenges us to dive into discerning God's longings for us in any particular time and circumstance. The Bible communicates God's greatest hopes and intentions for humanity. And while the Bible brings clarity, it is also filled with contradictions that many people have used to proof-text ideology, justify oppression, and otherwise weaponize faith. This is one of the most destructive and painful legacies of the Christian story that must always be lamented.

I do not believe in biblical literalism—the belief that the Bible is the exact word of God—for to understand a document written by humans that is fundamentally flawed as the inerrant word of God leads to proof-texting and dangerous misapplication. The Bible passages I use throughout this book come from the Common English Bible (CEB), a translation that does its best balancing direct translation and intent of the author. Ultimately, the Bible contains beautiful passages that evoke love, hope, joy, and peace, and it also contains the rawness and reality of a world filled with ugliness, despair, sorrow, and destruction. While some might prefer a faith devoid of difficulty, strife, and conflict, I find deep comfort in the fact that, in the midst of the good and the bad, God still speaks.

The Fourfold Jesus

> *I have become all things to all people, so I could save some by all possible means. All the things I do are for the sake of the gospel, so I can be a partner with it.* —1 Corinthians 9:22–23

One of the dangers of writing about Jesus is that we risk putting him in some kind of intellectual, theological, or cultural box. While this may be true for any topic, when it's about Jesus and the message of change that his presence brings, too often we want to either tame and domesticate him to fit our preferred version of the gospel or weaponize him to sustain and reinforce systems of marginalization and privilege. Sure, there is much space in between those two edges, but in either case, we must be wary that we don't mistake our individual preferences about how we want to live for the ways that Jesus models and teaches us how to live. We must resist the urge to use the life of Jesus to proof-text our own beliefs and actions, when the life and teachings of Jesus should be the foundation upon which our actions and beliefs are built.

It seems as if the more we narrow, confine, and simplify our understanding of Jesus, the more secure we feel. I would argue that the very nature of Jesus' lived expansiveness and unexpected disruptions shows that God understands the reality of the human condition and life in the everyday.

As we dive into definitions of Jesus the Prophet, Priest, Pastor, and Poet, let's begin with some questions that help us figure out what we think of Jesus. Consider which of these statements seems right to you:

A. Is Jesus a Prophet, a table-turning activist and political troublemaker who challenges us to express our righteous indignation with passion and courage?

B. Is Jesus a Priest, a going-off-to-pray miracle worker and spiritual teacher who offers us a way to connect with God?

C. Is Jesus a Pastor, a giving-the-benefit-of-the-doubt curator of relationships and bridge builder who yearns for us to cross cultural, economic, and theological divides?

D. Is Jesus a Poet, a more-questions-than-answers sculptor of words and actions, one who opens the human imagination to see possibilities for the world?

Like so many multiple-choice tests you took in high school, I believe the right answer is actually E: All of the Above.

Naturally, we tend to focus on the aspects of Jesus that we like and shy away from or reject those parts that challenge us. If we are activists, we likely focus on the prophetic nature of Jesus. If spiritual disciplines are our jam, we focus on the priestly aspects of Jesus. If relationships are the most important part of our faith life, then the pastoral Jesus is where we find connection. If we like using our imagination about what life could be, bring on Jesus the Poet! Expanding our understanding of Jesus might challenge us to consider who Jesus is calling us to be—and then we might have to adapt, change, and respond. Oh my!

This idea of the fourfold nature of Jesus—Prophet, Priest, Pastor, and Poet—is not new. It has roots in the writing of John Calvin, a French theologian who lived during the Protestant Reformation of the sixteenth century. In *Institutes of the Christian Religion,* he offers three "offices" of Jesus—Prophet, King, and Priest—as ways for us to understand humanity's relationships with Christ. The Prophet is about the truth of God (God's truths for humanity). The King is about protection of God (how humanity is cared for by God). The Priest is about connections to God (how humanity connects to God).[1] Even though I disagree with Calvinists a lot, these frames help me embrace the breadth of who Jesus is rather than focus only on the parts I like. Sure, we all gravitate toward one or two aspects of Jesus' life and teachings—a part of him with which we feel a special bond. But we must not do so to the extent of ignoring the other aspects of Jesus, who models for us the importance of holding in harmony many ways of moving through the world.

You will notice that Calvin has only three metaphors for Jesus. Calvin probably used king language for protector, not only in a

[1] Book II, Chapter 15, Section 1, https://www.ccel.org/ccel/calvin/institutes.iv.xvi.html

physical sense, but also in the well-being sense as a pastor does with their congregation. Ultimately, that is what the monarchy was supposed to do, protect and pastor their people. And as far as the "poet" goes, I am sure that I am not the first to believe Jesus was a poet. I don't remember when I started adding "poet," but I've always been struck by way that the creative elements of Jesus were often ignored. There are many books and articles with two or three of the P's and many with Calvin's triad, but as far as I can tell, not many with these four linked together. Again, I doubt I'm the first and count myself in good company with anyone else who has found this a helpful breakdown.

Okay, on to my take. How is Jesus Prophet, Priest, Pastor, and Poet?

The Prophetic Jesus is the activist, the one who wears passion and anger out in the open. The Prophet Jesus is filled with righteous indignation because humanity has lost sight of who God is calling us to become. Prophets do not predict the future of the world; they express to the world God's intentions for its future.

The Priestly Jesus tends to our connections to the Holy One, to God. He calls us to a life of prayer, reflection, worship, and spiritual discipleship. The Priestly Jesus reminds us to stay rooted in our divine connection and calling and to continue to follow the one who has called us. Jesus does this not out of a need for control but a yearning for us to also have integrity in what we do. This Priestly Jesus acknowledges the need to keep growing, learning, and inquiring because we are never done becoming what God intends. In many ways, the perfection of Jesus shows up in his willingness to admit his own imperfection and continue to learn, grow, and better follow the calling of the Spirit. Jesus the Priest helps us see and connect to God's guidance and growth, not our own.

The Pastoral Jesus challenges us to be in community, even and especially with those who are excluded, hated, or plain impossible to love. Jesus pushes us to reimagine what it means to offer a place of belonging. Relationships are not just about being nice, avoiding conflict, or sacrificing convictions to find commonality; rather, they mean seeing the other as divinely created, beautifully complex, and always in process. By following the Pastoral Jesus, we remember that other people are also created by and belong to God. Jesus the Pastor does not demand conformity and uniformity from those who claim to follow him, but rather empathy, compassion, and understanding.

And finally, the Poetic Jesus. Rather than pushing us toward a faith that is stifled, calcified, and boxed in, the Poet Jesus offers us a revelatory and expansive faith, fueled and fed by divine imagination. Jesus the Poet is not a beret-wearing hipster reciting spoken word in a darkened café. Then again, he could be. The Poet Jesus could also be the transgender soloist in a church, offering operatic beauty to the world. The Poet Jesus could be a bisexual Latinx living off the grid in a tiny home, challenging the world to rethink our relationship with the land, its people, and ourselves. The Poet Jesus could be the teenager hiking three miles into the desert with water, food, clothing, and medical supplies to help save the lives of migrants who are making the dangerous trek across the borderlands. The Poet Jesus could be the migrant making the dangerous trek across the borderlands. The Poet Jesus shows up at the church potluck, at the musical concert, through the latest smartphone app, in our alone time, and in places too numerous to count.

Are these the only images of Jesus? Surely not. But they are a place to start. Noticing these dimensions of Christ pushes us toward a nuanced and whole understanding of Jesus that provides a footing for future faith explorations. These images free us to think about who Jesus may be for each of us, rather than providing a confining narrative for who Jesus must be for everyone.

Putting Jesus into a theological, social, cultural, or behavioral box is exactly what conservative fundamentalist Christian traditions do. So let's not do that. Rather than using Jesus as a rigid litmus test for proofing and proving beliefs and behaviors, we must allow Jesus to guide us. Jesus, in all the beautiful breadth that is possible, leads us as we move together toward a more just, wise, and loving world.

We will dive deeper. I am such a proponent of this fourfold understanding of Jesus because holding this complexity challenges me to think more broadly about who Jesus is, what he did, what we are invited to do, and how we are called to be in the world. Making sure that I do not lose sight of all elements forces me not to be lazy and haphazard about my walk with Jesus Christ but to be emboldened and empowered by the breadth and expansiveness that is offered through him.

I will begin by establishing a foundation upon which these four ways of being are built. This lens of the Prophet, Priest, Pastor, and Poet invites us to think more broadly about the multiple natures of Jesus and to be changed and transformed by each nature. We are naturally drawn to the aspect of Jesus that most mirrors our own personality or preferences. I know that I lean toward Jesus the Prophet, the activist and the rabble-rouser, because I believe that protest is an essential aspect of most movements for change. It's taken me a while to appreciate how different people follow Jesus. But I've learned that being open to the fullness of the ways of Christ expands my understanding of the manifold nature of both Jesus and myself.

Here are a few biblical examples of how Jesus manifests these four ways of being:

Jesus the Prophet: In John 4, Jesus talks to a Samaritan woman at a well. At first glance, this seems to be a simple act of kindness. But given the systems that marginalized her because of her gender and social standing, this was an act of protest.

Jesus the Priest: In Matthew 14, just after he and the disciples somehow fed five thousand people (more like ten thousand if you include women and children), Jesus begins by going away to prayer and putting the confused disciples on a boat and ends with one of them being able to walk on water as Jesus did. This is not just about Jesus needing to take time to rest; it is about challenging the disciples not to revel in their own abilities to make miracles happen but to remain centered on the power of God.

Jesus the Pastor: Jesus is constantly inviting people into spaces of belonging and community. In Matthew 11, Jesus calls those who are weary and reminds them that in following him, and in belonging to this movement, they will find rest.

Jesus the Poet: Throughout scripture, Jesus answers accusations and questions with stories and more questions. This approach is not about abdicating responsibility or trying to shame somebody. He tells parables and poses questions to challenge humanity to think more expansively and creatively about faith.

I will be the first to admit that I am not always receptive to the challenge of embodying the multidimensional expressions of Jesus. In many aspects of my life, be it parenting my children, pastoring a church, or engaging in politics, I want to be prophetic when I really need to be pastoral, and sometimes a priestly posture is not as helpful as a poetic one. But I am always grateful for the many ways that Jesus challenges me to see the importance and interdependence of each way of being.

The Life and Teachings of Jesus

Back in the 1990s, there was a trend in the evangelical church in which people wore bracelets with "WWJD" on them. It stood for "What Would Jesus Do?" Many of us felt it was kind of a trite way to think about faith, as if wearing four letters on our wrists would magically bring to fruition all our hopes and dreams. Thinking back, I do think that perspective was probably a little condescending and accompanied a simplistic theology that lacked nuance and contextual rigor. Faith is often not as tidy as we want it to be. Jesus does offer us many teachings that are pretty simple in concept, if only to get more complicated in the application.

The Prophetic Jesus disrupts injustice when the woman accused of adultery by religious leaders is being unfairly judged. "They continued to question [Jesus], so he stood up and replied, 'Whoever hasn't sinned should throw the first stone.' Bending down again, he wrote on the ground. Those who heard him went away, one by one, beginning with the elders. Finally, only Jesus and the woman were left in the middle of the crowd" (John 8:7–9).

The Priestly Jesus is constantly just going off to pray. "Early in the morning, well before sunrise, Jesus rose and went to a deserted place where he could be alone in prayer" (Mark 1:35).

The Pastoral Jesus teaches that sometimes we need community to advocate for our healing. "Some people brought to him a man who was deaf and could hardly speak, and they begged him to place his hand on the man for healing" (Mark 7:32).

The Poetic Jesus is always inviting us to think beyond our imagination, like when he challenged the religious leaders about healing on the Sabbath. "When he said these things, all his opponents were put to shame, but all those in the crowd rejoiced at all the extraordinary things he was doing" (Luke 13:17).

I share these not as litmus tests we can use to develop "What would Jesus do?" purity rules, which Jesus' teachings have too often been relegated to. What I argue is that we must always consider context, intent, complexity, and nuance by stripping away the binaries and black-white thinking that permeate so much of our worldview. Going back to the "both/and," we must consider Jesus' teachings as both his earthly connection to humanity and part of how he gives humanity access to God. When we see Jesus' life and teaching as part of God's revealing of God's plan for humanity, and ultimately our divine relationship to God that we are promised in the existence of Jesus the Christ, our understanding of salvation and how we respond to that gift become richer, more textured, fuller, and ultimately more meaningful.

The Disruption and Death of Jesus

But the life and teaching of Jesus are only the beginning of our salvation journey. A crucial aspect of our calling to follow Christ is disruption, not for its own sake, but to see God's will be done here on earth as it is in heaven.

The life of Jesus was about disrupting the human understanding of evil and death and disrupting how death and evil manifest on earth in the form of empire, oppression, and destruction. Make no mistake, Jesus' disruption of those things was a calling to help reveal God's plans and intentions for humanity, and in response to those actions, he was executed. I do not believe that he had to die in order to connect us to God for eternity, but he understood that when power is challenged, even the most well-intentioned communities can turn to mobs and seek the death of one-time champions to protect power. This is what Jesus did. And this disruption and death, along with his life and teaching, are integral to understanding the breadth and depth of salvation through Christ.

I have always been surprised when some Christian traditions skip over the death and crucifixion of Jesus and head right to Easter and the empty tomb. In a world filled with so much pain and struggle and strife, I understand the urge to skip over sorrow and get to the good part. But the death of Jesus is the culmination of a life that challenged institutions of power, questioned authority, and rejected exclusionary norms—to the point where he was killed by those whose power he challenged. If we take the death of Jesus seriously, we must examine our own institutions, power, and norms and see if they too must be challenged. The death of Jesus shows us that anyone who brings attention to institutional sins or challenges the authority of the powerful risks suffering and death.

The killing of Christ is a mirror of what can happen when power is threatened, so we must not skip over it too quickly. If we do, we risk siding with the powers that Jesus stood against in the first place. The death of Christ also offers us a connection to God. While the death of Jesus was not a requirement for God's love, it provides a moment when God, through Christ, experiences the depth of human suffering. This moment joins us to God in a way that goes beyond any act or teaching of the living Christ. Jesus' death inextricably and eternally bonds humanity and God in a way that only shared death and suffering can do. Ultimately, the death of Christ, and the despair felt by those who believed in him, provided God with an opportunity to exhibit hope and new life.

The Atonement and Salvation of Jesus

Thankfully, the Jesus story does not end with death, for there is always hope and new life. We are resurrection people, after all. And I would argue that it is in the culmination of the life, death, and resurrection that salvation is freely offered to humanity.

Pause for a quick dive into some "theology you may not have asked for but is important to know."

You have probably heard the words *atonement* and *salvation*. While I am not going to dive into all the theories that exist, I want to be perfectly clear about what I believe to be true. There is no one right understanding of atonement (how the sins of humanity are absolved) or salvation (how humanity is eternally connected and saved as God's own). Far too many theories of atonement and salvation exist for me to tackle them here. Instead, I want to suggest to you that the life of Christ has just as much to say as his death and resurrection. The healing that Jesus offers to so many—the grace and forgiveness that he extends, the hope that he offers his followers—is too powerful for me to ignore. These were not acts of a mere mortal but divine revelations of new life, abundant hope, and eternal connection to the Divine.

Again, do not let anybody tell you that there is one correct belief about the atonement or salvation. Rather, find your footing in the resurrection because even when we do not know the hows or whys, God has promised that death and despair will not have the last word.

The Resurrection of Jesus Christ

So what about the resurrection of Jesus? I'll just get it out of the way and say that I believe in the bodily resurrection of Christ. I know, I know. You may not have expected that! I mean, I've been sounding like a thoughtful person, and now I'm admitting that I believe that a dead body can come back to life? Exactly.

It is important for you to understand this: I believe in the bodily resurrection not because of science or empirical evidence but because it is an outrageous and disruptive claim. It is an event beyond my imagination and beyond my human comprehension, and, if true, it turns upside down my assumptions about the future of the world. But it's that very fact—that it transcends everything I assume to be true or possible about how the world works—that gives me hope.

Working in concert, the life, death, and resurrection of Jesus talk back to so many indicators that suggest that death and destruction will have the last word, that the world is destined to crumble. The bodily resurrection of Christ gives me hope that, through the power of God, the world can become better. I choose to believe that the world will know healing beyond what I as a mere human can comprehend.

Salvation is about an eternity of connection to God. It is not about saving anyone from a lifetime of damnation. You do not need to believe that salvation is experienced solely and only through death on the cross; you need not see Jesus connecting us to God for eternity as some militaristic or conquering victory; and you certainly do not need to believe that salvation is the result of some divine parent sacrificing their child. What I offer to you is the possibility that salvation is an expression of love, an act of hope, and an unearned promise. Jesus didn't die just as a sacrifice for your sins; Jesus lived and was resurrected for the hope of your future. No matter how despairing and broken the world is, the life, death, and resurrection of Jesus promise that we are connected to God for eternity and that hope, joy, love, and peace will have the final word. In gratitude for this promise, we worship and serve God in our lives and the world.

The Possibility and Pursuit of Jesus

Again, the "So what?" is that we must always see the resurrection as the ultimate vision of possibility that God offers us in Jesus. In Jesus we are offered a different way for the world to be. This is not the way that you or I want the world to be, but how together you and I discern God's intentions for us and the world and visions of what that might be, beyond our own imagination.

This also means that we choose to pursue this possibility and collaborate in the revealing of those intentions for the world. It means that we choose to wrestle with and follow those teachings that Jesus lays out before us so that we may help to tease out the possibilities that God may have for the world. And it means that we choose to believe—in some audacious, ridiculous, even foolish way—in some form of the possibility of resurrection, that even out of despair and death, there is the possibility of hope and new life.

Now I want to be very clear here. I do not believe that belief in Jesus is the only way to meet God or the only way to salvation. While I don't believe that Jesus is the only way for everyone, he is a life-giving, beautiful, and worthwhile way for me and many others. In Jesus, I find a pure and powerful calling to be a human worthy of the love God has promised me. Through Jesus' life, death, and resurrection, I am connected to God now and forever. So for me, Jesus is the way.

Choosing faith each day, for me, means claiming Jesus as my ultimate guide, teacher, sojourner, comrade, collaborator, and accomplice. Jesus provides a complex and complete example of how I strive to live in the world. Some Christian traditions seek to motivate through obligation, shame, and guilt. Following Jesus in those ways seems exhausting, miserable, and demotivating. Rather, because of the depth of humanity that Jesus experienced, the divinity in which he lived, and the unimaginable act of coming back to life, in gratitude and joy I choose Jesus because he offers me the possibility for a world better than what I can imagine or accomplish on my own:

A world where injustice is righted.

A world where curiosity is encouraged.

A world where belonging is known.

A world where abundance is shared.

What I hope you gain from this book and from wrestling with these images of Jesus is that you find more than one possible way to address the many struggles in the world, and maybe ones that others cannot envision themselves. I hope that in seeing this vision for the world, you feel compelled and called to pursue it. Most importantly, we don't all need to see the same possibilities for each and every struggle of the world, but if we collectively imagine a world that is infinitely better than what it is today, the world will change.

This sounds nice in concept but ridiculous in reality. But then so does the resurrection.

The Beckoning and Becoming of Jesus

Okay, if you are still with me, you believe in the possibility that is offered in the life, death, and resurrection of Christ, and some part of you is feeling compelled to pursue that reality for yourself, your community, and the world. So now comes the difficult part: not just "So what?" but "How do we do it?" Because at some point, even God's greatest hopes and intentions for humanity must be manifested into reality. We must now be that which we claim to want to become in light of the possibilities laid out before us. No problem.

This is where the work becomes real. This is when our ideas—theological, ideological, or political—have real-life implications, and we must decide if they are worth pursuing and putting energy behind, making them come into being. Becoming that which God hopes and intends is difficult because the nature of institutions and individuals is to grasp tightly to power, influence, and wealth by leaning into suspicion, security, and self-preservation. This is not always a bad thing, but sometimes what God hopes for us will create conflict as it did when Jesus was called to challenge the power of his day. Of course, I do not wish for anyone to give up their life, but I do hope that folks understand that being beckoned toward these possibilities of hope and new life is powerful and profound and often turns what we know as normal and comfortable upside down.

We must not enter into this stage of our faith lightly. It is daunting because the chasms and breaches of the world are daunting. I certainly do not want to minimize that reality, but something we must always remember and take comfort in is that we are not called into this work alone. This book focuses on the plurality of the nature of Christ—prophetS, priestS, pastorS, and poetS—because being and becoming the resurrected Christ is not an individualized endeavor, it is a communal one.

Okay, so there you have it, the foundations for this invitation to get to know Jesus in a new and familiar (but hopefully expanded) way. Now, my dear prophets, priests, pastors, and poets, let's get to being and becoming the resurrected Christ.

The Prophetic Jesus

Put the sword back into its place. All those who use the sword will die by the sword. —Matthew 26:52

12 Ways to Know You Might Vibe with the Prophetic Jesus

- Your soul sings when you are part of a public action.
- You naturally excel at helping people understand the meaning, importance, and purpose of public protest and direct action.
- You nerd out about protest chants, and you have strong opinions them.
- You are always prepared to disrupt and clear space so that voices traditionally silenced or excluded have a chance to be heard and seen.
- An ideal retreat would be a nonviolent direct-action training.
- You never pass up a chance to honk in support of a picket line or freeway overpass gathering.
- It annoys and enrages you when people say about protest, "People would be more likely to listen if they were not so inconvenienced".

- In your bag right now, you have the number of a lawyer in case you get arrested at a protest, markers in case you need to make a sign, a whistle for street actions, or a mask in case some tear gas is in your future.
- Others affirm your passion and perseverance.
- You are often misunderstood as too aggressive, angry, or antagonistic.
- You want people to remember that institutions are built for self-preservation, so change is only sparked and instigated by disruption and discomfort.
- Your greatest hope for the church is to have the courage to be the church it claims to be, even at the risk of its own death.

Jesus as Prophet

A table-turning activist, political troublemaker, and cultural provocateur who challenges the world to align with God's hopes with righteous indignation, passion, and courage.

The Prophetic Jesus

This may be a strange way to start the section on the Prophet Jesus, but I begin by talking about meetings. In my life of working in the church, I have been to so many meetings. As I think back to all the sizes and scopes of meetings I have been to, it feels like a terrible telling of *The Cat in the Hat: The Meeting Version:*

- Will you meet around a table?
- Will you meet when all are able?
- Will you meet with a small group?
- Will you meet to just create more hoops?
- Will you meet with your friends?
- Will these meetings ever end?

At my best I listen, pay attention, and stay attuned to the passions and perspectives that each person brings to the setting, large or small.

At my worst, which honestly is most of the time, I am incredibly impatient, slightly condescending, and eager to get on to the next item of business. Okay, I lied. At my worst, I get *super*-annoyed when we begin to talk about a subject for the umpteenth time and the same person gets up to say the same thing they have always said before. It usually has to do with an important issue, too: climate change, militarism, immigration, etc. All laudable things, but I just want them to sit down and stop already.

You see, the worst.

But here's the thing: When I am honest with myself and reflect on what it means to be prophetic in the world as exemplified in scripture, this is how most prophets are perceived: annoying, pesky, aggressive, not-knowing-when-to-stop-talking...you get it. Prophets are often the ones screaming God's truth into spaces where people desperately need to hear it.

To be prophetic is not to tell the future but simply to speak God's hopes for the world into the world. Sometimes that message is reinforced by warnings about what may happen should we not listen. These warnings are not meant to terrorize or scare, but to prompt us to change paths in order to allow God's intentions to have a chance to be revealed. Prophets are rarely celebrated by the masses because it is usually the masses who have fallen into the traps of power that work against God's intentions. And prophets seldom self-identify as prophets because to be a prophet is a calling that no one would want. It is a life of isolation, rejection, and danger because you must speak a truth that no one wants to hear. Prophets are called to disrupt normalcy, comfort, and security, and rarely is a disruptive act celebrated.

It could be argued that the Prophet Jesus is an overarching lens through which he lived his entire life and that each of Jesus' four natures disrupts the norm in some way: The Priest disrupts the norm of disconnection, the Pastor disrupts the norm of individuality, and the Poet disrupts the norm of indifference. However, in this chapter, I will focus on the aspects of the Prophet that are about the disruption of injustice, power, and empire. I do this not only because of the context of the day, but precisely because of the above reality that each of the other three natures will also carry some level of disruption on its own.

The Prophet Jesus, out of hope and love for humanity, does all he can to remind us of God's hopes for us all, and he wants us to do the same.

How Jesus Shows Up as a Prophet

The go-to scripture passage when people speak of Jesus the prophet is when he turns over the tables in Matthew 21:12–13. "Then Jesus went into the temple and threw out all those who were selling and buying there. He pushed over the tables used for currency exchange and the chairs of those who sold doves. He said to them, 'It's written, *My house will be called a house of prayer.* But you've made it a hideout for crooks.'" While this is an important moment, I think it is too narrow a view of what it means to be prophetic. Too often, prophets get pigeonholed as angry and aggressive so can be easily dismissed. But Jesus was not only about turning over tables. He also spoke God's disruptive truth and realities in other ways that were just as meddling and uncomfortable.

Almost every time the disciples make some assumptions about a person or a situation, Jesus has to remind them that God may indeed have different intentions.

- In Matthew 14:15, the disciples want to send the people away, saying, "This is an isolated place and it's getting late. Send the crowds away so they can go into the villages and buy food for themselves." But Jesus disrupts their visions of scarcity to remind them that God may have different intentions for both the disciples and the crowd: "There's no need to send them away. You give them something to eat" (v. 16).
- In John 4, Jesus goes to the well and talks to the Samaritan woman, and "Jesus' disciples arrived and were shocked that he was talking with a woman" (v. 27). They bought into the cultural idea of gender roles and cultural appropriateness, but Jesus disrupted that norm to show that God had different intentions and hopes for the woman when she "put down her water jar

and went into the city. She said to the people, 'Come and see a man who has told me everything I've done! Could this man be Christ?'" (vv. 28–29).

- When one of those who was with Jesus when he was arrested tried to defend him, Jesus chose nonviolence instead. "One of those with Jesus reached for his sword. Striking the high priest's slave, he cut off his ear. Then Jesus said to him, 'Put the sword back into its place. All those who use the sword will die by the sword'" (Matthew 26:51–52). Jesus disrupts the idea that we respond to violence with violence.

Those poor disciples are constantly used as examples of not understanding God's intentions. But they are not the only ones unable to see beyond their own realities, forcing Jesus to step in. When the powerful come at Jesus, trying to trick him, he does not allow them to set the boundaries of what can be. Instead, he lets them know that the bounds of what can be are set by God alone.

- In Matthew 12, when the religious leaders question Jesus about working and healing on the Sabbath, a cultural and religious no-no, Jesus uses their own texts and practices to call out their hypocrisy and point them toward God's intentions and hopes for those who need healing.
- In John 8, when church leaders bring a woman to be stoned for adultery in order to test Jesus, he reminds them that it is God's job to pass judgment, not humanity's. He disrupts the idea that humanity gets to be the arbiter and distributor of grace, a gift only God can bestow.
- And at the end of his life, when he had pushed the empire to the brink and was given a chance to save his own life, he did not succumb to the influence and temptation put before him by the power around him. He disputed the idea that one's calling and values could be purchased for the cost of one's integrity, passion, and in this case, life.

Again, the Prophet Jesus shows up through all four of these elements because all four are meant to disrupt ways that we might limit our understanding of God's hopes and intentions.

Ultimately, the Prophet Jesus is here for us because too often there are times—whether in grief, complacency, or willful ignorance to avoid the pains of the world—we forget the promises made and lose sight of hope. The Prophet Jesus reminds us that it is God's intention for us to know hope, love, peace, and joy and that it is through Jesus, the ultimate disruptor and prophetic witness, that reality is made known.

How Prophets Show Up in the World

Just as humans exist in the world in diverse cultures and contexts, there are diverse ways in which humans express prophetic witness in the world. So we must be careful that we do not fall into the trap of limiting our definition of what it means to be "prophetic" to a few narrow understandings. When we do this, not only do we risk litmus-testing and gatekeeping for some artificial collective, we limit the expansive ways God's hopes and intentions can disrupt that which is wrong in the world.

Here are a few ways I have experienced prophets in the world, as reflected in the fourfold Jesus and keeping in mind the definition "a table-turning activist, political troublemaker, and cultural provocateur who challenges the world to align with God's hopes with righteous indignation, passion, and courage."

Prophet in handcuffs: I believe that nonviolent direct action is a deeply profound and powerful act of prophetic disruption that one can engage in. To be clear, not everyone should or can risk arrest. The ability to engage in civil disobedience and risk arrest is highly contextual and should not be ranked as better or more worthy than other prophetic acts. Civil disobedience disrupts the idea of retaliating with terror and force and demands that those with power acknowledge the humanity in the ones standing before them and ultimately make different choices.

Priestly prophet in the system: Depending on the season of my own life, I have been both frustrated and deeply moved by those who see worth in institutions and the stability that they can provide. The priestly prophet understands that no institution is perfect, nor will it naturally move toward flexibility and self-reflection without being held accountable. The priestly prophet holds up a mirror to an institution to make sure it stays true to who it has said it is and wants to become. This may be done in quiet or loud ways but can be dangerous and risky to one's livelihood and reputation.

Pastoral prophet with the people: The pastoral prophet, quite frankly, is annoying because they are constantly disrupting the idea that our "enemies" are unworthy of dignity and empathy. They often challenge communities to be the body that they claim to be and not the body that the world wants them to be. The pastoral prophets take seriously Romans 12:14, "Bless people who harass you—bless and don't curse them." You see, it's annoying.

Poetic prophet on the walls: The poetic prophet compels us to believe in the ridiculously possible without using words. Whether it is melody that tugs at our soul, a painting that reaches deeply into a well of emotion we didn't know existed, or a mural on a wall that challenges the world to see an injustice of the day, the poetic prophet disrupts our tendency to normalize that which should not be normalized and shocks us into seeing injustice that need to be seen and the healing that we are not able to see on our own.

And while I do caution against thinking that being prophetic is all and only about table overturning, in some ways, being prophetic is exactly all about turning over the damn tables. The expansive part of it requires that in doing so, we remember that we may all engage in the act differently depending on our context, capacity, ability, and season of life. That's the beauty of creation.

Being and Becoming Prophets

As I mentioned in the preface, at the writing of this book, it feels like the United States is on the precipice of civil war and authoritarianism. I wish this was hyperbole and hope it does not come to fruition. I also hope the trend toward Christian nationalism has not become so deeply rooted that we will not be able to extricate ourselves from it.

For this reason, I believe each of us and our communities must take seriously the commitment to being and becoming prophets in the world, disrupting that which needs to be disrupted, and lifting up what we see as God's hopes and intentions for humanity. This is no longer a time to only think, pray, and discern, but those faithful acts must lead us to action in all ways so that our faith can make a difference in the world.

To be and become prophetic requires that we figure out what that means for each of us. For some of us it will look like public action, while for others it will be letter-writing and phone calls, and still for others it will be supporting those who are on the streets. These are all aspects of what it means to disrupt the idea that we are alone in this struggle, when the resurrection is the greatest reminder that we are not.

10 Ways to Become the Prophet God Intends You to Be

1. If you pray for the poor and the oppressed in worship, make sure those words are backed up with genuine and demonstrable actions. Be the church you claim to be, and disrupt the idea that the church is all talk and no action.
2. If you want to immediately affect people's lives, engage in direct mutual aid and disrupt the idea that the only way people can be supported is if they can access and navigate complex structures and institutions.
3. If you want to make sure you do not become an echo chamber of belief and stagnation, develop a culture of healthy disagreement and self-reflection, disrupting the assumption that "once on the right side of justice, always on the right side of justice."
4. If you want people to take the church seriously, show up at protests, marches, town halls, and other public actions and disrupt the idea that faith communities are absent from the public discourse or unwilling to take a stand.

5. If you want to build for community longevity, collaborate with organizations that are already doing the work and disrupt the idea that your church should be in charge, lead, or even be named at every event, gathering, or action.
6. If you want to avoid burnout, step away for occasional times of rest, renewal, and re-creation and disrupt the idea that martyrdom is a sign of worth and commitment.
7. If you want to avoid falling into the trap of individualism and buy into the belief that any one of us can topple injustice on our own, participate in community organizing and public actions where you are not leading but following.
8. If you want to be part of breaking cycles of retribution, revenge, and violence, commit to nonviolence and disrupt the idea that you must repay force with force, dehumanization with dehumanization, or evil acts with evil acts.
9. If you want to be sure that what you do matters, make sure to engage, be in conversation, and develop relationships with those who are directly impacted and disrupt the scourge of disconnected saviorism that so many carry.
10. If you want to keep expanding in your prophetic purpose, integrate your public action into worship and study (priestly), communal interaction (pastoral), and creative outlets (poetic) and disrupt the idea that the only reason one can show up as a prophet is to turn over tables in the street.

For the Body, Mind, and Spirit of the Prophets

A table-turning activist, political troublemaker, and cultural provocateur who challenges the world to align with God's hopes with righteous indignation, passion, and courage.

For Personal Reflection and Movement

- When you picture the prophetic people in your life, who do you see?
- When was the last time you were unapologetically prophetic?

- What barriers, obstacles, or variables hold you back from being prophetic?
- Talk about a time when you felt being prophetic was too risky.
- How do you handle conflict with friends, family, and community members when your prophetic witness creates discomfort or conflict?

For Communal Reflection and Movement

- When has your community been its most prophetic?
- When has your community struggled with being prophetic?
- Are there communities we claim to support in word but have hesitated to support in action publicly for fear of the conflict it might cause?

Prayers for the Prophets

Let us pray…

One: God of the disruptors, the protestors,

ALL: the whistleblowers, the system changers,

One: those unafraid to speak truth, those willing to make the dinner table uncomfortable,

ALL: and those who speak aloud God's hopes for the world when the world does not want to hear, we come to you in prayer.

One: In a world that chooses silence in the face of injustice.

ALL: God, hear our prayer.

One: Allow us each the courage to find our prophetic voices, hold tenderly our anxieties, and act as we each are called.

ALL: God, hear our prayer.

One: If there are places in our community where we need to be reminded of and redirected towards your hopes and intentions, grant us courage and confidence to change.

ALL: God, hear our prayer.

One: In a world overcome with destruction, terror, and hatred, may we find our prophetic role of healing, hope, and love.

ALL: God, hear our prayer.

One: God, whether the prophetic voices ring out from inside or outside of this community,

ALL: grant us courage to hear. Amen.

The Priestly Jesus

Sit here while I pray. —Mark 14:32

12 Ways to Know You Might Vibe with the Priestly Jesus

- Your soul sings when a group of people collaborate on crafting a prayer for worship that comes directly from their experiences.
- You naturally excel at helping people understand that we focus on our inward spiritual growth because of our commitment to an effective outward expression of faith.
- You nerd out about seeing biblical texts in the original form.
- You are always prepared to lead people in *lectio* or *visio divina.*
- Your ideal retreat would be a silent one.
- You love the idea and practice of weekly communion in worship you never pass up a chance to pray.
- You are perplexed by those who think that pausing for prayer is "unproductive" or something to get over.
- In your bag or on an app you have a timer, a chime, or bell.
- Others affirm your ability to help groups center in the midst of chaos or conflict.

- You are often misunderstood as not political enough, slow to action, or uncommitted.
- One thing you want people to remember is that their current faith is deeply rooted in the faith of their ancestors and their faith will be the roots of their descendants' faith.
- Your greatest hope for the church is to find a harmony between its inward and outward expressions of faith.

Jesus as Priest

A going-off-to-pray miracle worker and spiritual teacher who curates holy spaces, nurtures spiritual discipline, tends our histories, and invites us into ritual as ways to connect to God.

The Priestly Jesus

Early in my pastoral career, I was elected to high office in my denominational home, the Presbyterian Church (U.S.A.). At thirty-nine, I was a successful church planter, one of the early adopters of digital ministry, and a frequent speaker at conferences and events all over the country. I was riding high, especially in my own mind.

I was reminded of this after a particular event in the late 2000s. I was speaking at an event and found myself sharing the lineup with well-respected theologian and author Barbara Brown Taylor. Now Barbara Brown Taylor is one of those authors and speakers whose writing and speaking are simply captivating. She can craft words and images together that speak to your soul and help folks expand their understanding and expression of the Divine. After the event, all of the speakers were hanging out, and she came up to me and simply said three words: "Bruce, slow down." "You slow down, Barbara Brown Taylor." No, I didn't say that, but I may have initially thought it.

To be honest, these words, while unsolicited, were offered not with judgment or condescension, but with genuine compassion and care. She was not accusing me of being irresponsible or thoughtless but encouraging me to undertake more time and tending to all that I was doing. I was moving so quickly from event to event, from question to question, and from idea to idea that I was not giving the Spirit enough time to settle in my soul and provide my heart and mind clarity. Her prodding had nothing to do with energy level or personality; she just thought I should take seriously the call to communicate the gospel and to give myself every chance of doing it as fully as possible. Of course, I may be reading into her words way more than she intended, but that's what I heard, and it changed the way I have approached ministry ever since.

It is important to remember that the Priestly Jesus is not about slowing down, stepping away, and stopping all activity. The Priestly Jesus encourages us to slow down so we can take time to breathe in and out, remember where we come from, remember who will follow us, tether ourselves to those things that will guide us through the storms, and engage in ritual to remind ourselves to whom we belong.

The priestly aspect of Jesus emphasizes grounding in spiritual tradition, discipline, and ritual. This takes place in worship, communal prayer (from intercessory to confessional and thanksgiving), sacraments (baptism, communion), and other spiritual disciplines (study, *lectio divina,* etc.). Observing these traditions deepens our roots in long-standing communal wisdom—linking us to generations before and after. The Priestly Jesus challenges communities to make ritual not merely obligatory or habitual, but meaningful and compelling, so that faith feels essential and not transactional or commodified. Knowing that faith is a multigenerational endeavor, the Priestly Jesus also remembers that our current faith is clothed in the recognition of how its practices and commitments will impact future generations.

Essentially, the Priestly Jesus wants us to build up our outward expressions of faith by strengthening our inward individual and communal spiritual health—making space for spiritual introspection, resilience, and sustenance. And while there are no guarantees of outcomes, when we remember to stay grounded and connected, we ensure that other prophetic, pastoral, and poetic endeavors are that much more grounded, connected, and, hopefully, meaningful.

How Jesus Shows Up as a Priest

I will probably spend more time on this "How Jesus Shows Up" than any other because this is where Jesus offers the most direct examples of how to tend to your spiritual life. Not only does Jesus invite us to a life of prayer and contemplation, but he also consistently connects us to our past so we may move forward informed by the faithfulness of those who came before us. Finally, Jesus invites us into a life of ritual and sacrament, which for the Christian life is essential in order to stay inwardly grounded for our outward ministry.

The most obvious way that Jesus shows up is when he does some form of "going off to pray," which happens on numerous occasions. After he and the disciples fed the ten thousand, rather than throw a celebratory after-party or hold a debrief, he went off to pray by himself (Matthew 14:23, Mark 6:46). Just before choosing the twelve apostles, "Jesus went out to the mountain to pray, and he prayed to God all night long" (Luke 6:12). And then in Gethsemane, "Jesus and his disciples came to a place called Gethsemane. Jesus said to them, 'Sit here while I pray'" (Mark 14:32).

The Priestly Jesus shows up in other disciplines besides prayer. Jesus also reminds us of our deep multiplicity of interconnections, engages us in ritual, and challenges us to grow into a deeper understanding of God's intentions for our lives. The story of Mary and Martha (Luke 10:38–42) is a lovely example of being invited into a time of deeper relationship with God. "The Lord answered, 'Martha, Martha, you are worried and distracted by many things. One thing is necessary. Mary has chosen the better part. It won't be taken away from her'" (vv. 41–42). Now we must be careful when interpreting this scripture not to see this as an ultimate rebuke of Martha or to focus too much on two sisters (and women) being pitted against one another. Rather, Jesus reminds us that even the best of us can become distracted at times and may need to be invited in again and again to connect with the One who calls us to the journey of faith.

The Priestly Jesus also reminds us over and over again that we are connected to our past and our ancestors. Jesus reminds the people of his day, for political and cultural reasons, that we do not do what we do without reason or guidance. We follow the way that was paved by those who came before us and who gave us language and examples for how we are to pave the way for future generations.

I already laid out my understanding of the Bible in the introduction, but let me add that when linking back to the Hebrew scriptures and Jesus, we must be careful about how we understand the relationship between the Hebrew text and the gospels. Because many Jews do not believe that the Messiah has returned, it is important not to unintentionally use Hebrew texts in a way that suggests that the Jews have been saved by Jesus. There is much controversy within the Jewish community about this, but in my opinion and for the sake of my interfaith relationships, I firmly believe this is not for me to decide, so I am very careful not to use scripture in this way.

That said, scripture is scattered with Jesus referring to the Hebrew texts, directly and indirectly:

- During his time in the wilderness being tested and tempted for forty days, he quotes the Hebrew scriptures three times. In Matthew 4:4, Jesus cites Deuteronomy 8:3, saying, "It's written, 'People won't live only by bread, but by every word spoken by God.'" In 4:7, he cites Deuteronomy 6:16: "Again it's written, 'Don't test the Lord your God.'" Finally, in 4:10, he drops the mic as he quotes from Deuteronomy 6:13, "Go away, Satan, because it's written, 'You will worship the Lord your God and serve only him.'"
- In Matthew 19:18–19, after being asked by the rich young man what it would take to enter heaven, Jesus refers to the Ten Commandments: "Then Jesus said, 'Don't commit murder. Don't commit adultery. Don't steal. Don't give false testimony. Honor your father and mother, and love your neighbor as you love yourself.'"
- In Matthew 5:38–39, he references what people knew from the Hebrew law in order to contradict it for their time. "You have heard that it was said, 'An eye for an eye and a tooth for a tooth.'

But I say to you that you must not oppose those who want to hurt you. If people slap you on your right cheek, you must turn the left cheek to them as well."

- When Jesus meets the Samaritan woman at the well, he responds to her mention of her ancestor Jacob in a way that shows he understands her history and context: "'You aren't greater than our father Jacob, are you? He gave this well to us, and he drank from it himself, as did his sons and his livestock.' Jesus answered, 'Everyone who drinks this water will be thirsty again, but whoever drinks from the water that I will give will never be thirsty again. The water that I give will become in those who drink it a spring of water that bubbles up into eternal life'" (John 4:12–14).

The final and possibly the primary way that the Priestly Jesus shows up in the world is through the invitation of ritual, in recognized and official sacraments as well as more organic acts of communal connection. Rituals, at their most meaningful, are not just about the words or going through the motions. Rather, they make real a deep understanding of who God is and how God connects to every one of us in a different way. They speak to our souls and to the very nature of who we are as created beings. They speak to the ultimate things of God—sacred truths that defy human understanding and define how we are to be in relationship with God and with one another. Rituals renew our spirits and nurture our relationship with the Divine.

Rituals can and should be deeply contextual. Most churches and communities have rituals that may not even be understood as such.

- In the church of my childhood, Trinity Presbyterian Church in Stockton, California, at the end of the service we would all gather in a circle around the sanctuary and sing "Seek Ye First" as our closing song every Sunday.
- The church that I helped to start in San Francisco, Mission Bay Community Church, didn't pass an offering plate. Instead, we had folks come forward, and as one "offering" option they could take a card listing a task that the church needed help with that week.

- I have seen pastors sing children to the front, name by name like a teacher taking roll call (amazing—and no pressure on the next pastor).
- Rituals of giving Star Words on Epiphany, burning ashes on Ash Wednesday, various Good Friday rituals, or integrated cultural celebrations in worship help bring special days to life in new ways.

Rituals are ways that individuals and communities can connect more deeply to the Divine, so they should reflect the needs of the individuals and community that they are meant to serve.

Lastly, let me talk a bit about the importance of the sacraments, two rituals that were instituted by Jesus. A good general definition of a sacrament is this: an act that has been instituted or enacted by God in the past and that we commit to expressing today. The Catholic Church has seven sacraments: baptism, holy communion, reconciliation (or confession), confirmation, marriage, holy orders, and anointing of the sick. In many other Christian traditions, there are just two: baptism and communion, which is sometimes known as the eucharist or the Lord's supper. Both baptism and communion were instituted by Jesus, and they are signs that God is present on earth. As gatherers who worship God and are called together around the person known as Jesus, we see rituals as a sign of God's presence and an outward expression of an inward commitment. Baptism is a way to communally acknowledge that God has claimed us as God's own. Communion is the outward and communal expression of remembering that we are one in Christ and that Christ lived, died, and was resurrected for humanity. The ultimate power of rituals and sacraments is that they connect us to each other and to God.

So in all of these ways, the Priestly Jesus invites, prods, and challenges us to stay grounded in our faith and to do so in many ways: through prayer, through our traditions, and through our rituals. These foundational actions in turn provide concrete examples, practices, and disciplines that keep us connected to God, the One who promises new life when the world tries to convince us otherwise.

How Priests Show Up in the World

Much like Jesus, we must encourage the world to take time to connect to holy inwardness in order to give grounding and strength to our outward expression of faith. Too often we are characterized as being holed away and absent from the world, when in reality we are doing our part to remind the world to stay connected, integrated, and grounded.

Robust prayer life shows up in so many ways in the world. Prayer is a conversation with God and can take forms as diverse as the voices who are part of the conversation. In prayer, we all have different roles at different times. Sometimes we listen, and sometimes we respond. Sometimes others need to hear words of encouragement; at other times, silence is the most powerful prayer that can be offered. In prayer, God, too, responds in as many ways as we may pray to God. Sometimes prayer is one way: we talk and God listens. Other times we are the listener, silencing ourselves long enough to hear from God and detect the movement of the Spirit. Exactly how you pray is up to you. Some folks engage in a regular discipline of prayer at a particular time each day, while others see prayer as more spontaneous and interwoven with our activities during the day. I think a healthy prayer life includes both. We should all set aside some time to focus our body, heart, and mind on listening for God; we also need to be open to the moments when we simply need to talk to God or God needs to talk with us. No matter how or how much we pray, we can rest in the knowledge that God is paying attention. God's capacity to hold and respond to all things is far greater than ours. God responds to us in surprising and mysterious ways.

Staying connected to our past is about paying attention to scripture, tradition, and the people who helped form our faith. It is important not to worship those prepared the way for us, but to hold them tenderly as guides and fellow sojourners upon whose missteps and celebrations we can build our own journeys of faith.

Adding to more of my perspective on the Bible, to be a priestly people we must also read, embody, and express our holy text as a living, breathing container of God's voice to us and not as an old-fashioned, out-of-date relic of the faith. The Priestly Jesus reinforces the belief that the Bible acts as a sign of the depth and breadth of God's presence yesterday, today, and always.

With the same rigor that we approach scripture, we must examine tradition in order to discern what to leave behind and what to hold on to. When the COVID-19 pandemic hit in 2020, who could have guessed how quickly so many traditional churches would pivot to being church in new ways? Prior to the pandemic, conversations about screens in the sanctuary, recorded music, no bulletins, online giving, or virtual gatherings would have taken decades for congregations and caused mini-strokes for many members. But in 2020, within weeks, congregations had simply figured it out. All of a sudden, people were recording music and sermons, slideshows were assembled, people were preaching and praying via videoconference from across the country, and the church remained more than alive. While it was an exhausting time, people found their creative juices, creativity was unleashed, people leaned on one another to offer expertise, and most importantly, they examined the traditions of worship to decide what was truly important. What parts of worship needed to happen and what parts didn't became clear. Many congregations soon discovered that prayer, communion, music, reflections, and seeing one another's faces were the most important aspects. Gone were the details we may have fought about before: the logistics of offering, friendship pads, typos in the bulletin, and so much more. While I do not believe there are silver linings to that season of life, we did learn much about ourselves, namely that not all traditions need to stay and not every tradition should be let go.

When it comes to the ancestors who raised us and formed our faith, they bring a wealth of lived experiences. Their stories are wide-ranging and come from people who have always been on this land as well as those who arrived from another land—either by force, choice, or circumstance. And just as we examine scripture and traditions with nuance and care, we must also hold the complexity of every human who helped to shape and form our faith with tenderness and love. We must not make the mistake of lifting any one human being up to the point of idolatry, as every human who is part of our faith journey can offer us lived and expressed wisdom of both caution and curiosity. I am not sure there is much to say here other than this: To be priestly when connecting with the ancestors of the faith requires honesty in our assessment, grace, and our gratitudes, so we may in turn learn from all three.

The final two ways that we are priestly in the world are through the sacraments of baptism and communion. These two are central and vital to our experience and expression of Christianity. Let's first tackle baptism. Just as other cultures and faith traditions have rituals that celebrate welcome and renewal, Christianity provides one more perspective through which these are experienced in the world. There is no shortage of theological hot takes and opinions about baptism: how it's done, what it means, what words you use, what happens once it happens, etc. What I share is how I understand baptism and my hope for how it is presented to the world. First off, to be abundantly clear, being baptized is not a requirement to be seen, known, or loved by God. Full disclaimer: I love me some baptisms. I baptized all three of my children, and it was the honor of my ministry to do so. When I baptize children, the act of a community committing to raise that child feels powerful and spirit-shaking. When I baptize adults, the commitment to seeing the world through a new lens is inspiring and transforming. In baptism, we are claimed and named. Baptism is the tender act of a community saying to a child or an adult that they are special and that they belong: not in a "better than other people" kind of way but in a "beyond anything we could ever imagine" kind of belonging.

Being baptized means publicly claiming our place with the cloud of witnesses and the body of Christ. Again, baptism is not a ticket into these communities. You get no special privileges (parking spot or cuts at the coffee line), but the reciprocal and public nature of the ritual challenges the individual and community to hold one another with loving accountability and committed encouragement. When an adult is baptized, a community of faith says, "You have now made the decision to declare that you are part of this body called together by Christ." When an infant is baptized, the community says, "Those who have made the decision on your behalf have brought you into this body called together by Christ." In both cases, through baptism we are connected to one another beyond our earthly understandings and joined together with our ancestors, those present with us now, and those to come for eternity.

Baptism reminds us that we are not on this journey alone. Through baptism we vow that in the body of Christ—local and global—we will do this thing called faith together. Ultimately baptism is simply a response to and recognition of a relationship already promised by God. It's a calling to enter a new way of being in a relationship with God, not a guarantee for any kind of exchange with God. Baptism is not transactional. It is a public expression of our commitment to God and the community of faith and an acknowledgment of God's commitment to us.

And lastly, communion, or what some folks know as the Lord's supper or the eucharist. Communion is a celebration of a people gathered, a people nourished, and a people promised hope in the future. In communion, like in baptism, we're reminded that we are on this journey together. We remember that, no matter how difficult, frustrating, or tiresome the path may become, God nourishes us in body, mind, and soul.

When we share communion, something special occurs. We gather around a virtual or physical table that has been made expansive and sacred because Christ has invited us into a relationship that is not bound by the limitations of human understanding of community. The table is a place to which we are invited to unapologetically bring our whole selves: our culture, contexts, loves, hates, joys, sorrows, struggles, and celebrations. In communion, we hold one another with the love that God offers us. We are given permission to let go of all the analyses, assessments, and judgments that we bring to most interactions. Communion calls us to be vulnerable, open, and willing to see one another as the beautifully created human beings that we are. There are very few places where we can experience this reality. The communion table is the place we come closest to seeing one another with the purity and love with which God sees us every day.

When we come to the communion table, the bread reminds us that Christ is still among us: in death and in life. In the breaking and sharing of the bread, we remember that we are the body of Christ. We suffer together, and we are fed together. And when we share in the cup, we receive a new promise: that Jesus will come again, in some form, in some way. (Also: not our job to figure out the exact timing or form.) In that promise, we are given hope that someday there will be a new and better world. The cup of the new promise is about moving from this world into the next. When we drink it, we celebrate the promise that someday Christ will return and usher in a new creation, a new life, and a new way of being.

In many ways, all four forms of Jesus show up at the table. The Priest invites us into the ritual, and the Prophet, Poet, and Pastor disrupt and expand the very notion of what welcome, inclusion, and belonging can look like in the world. I believe the most welcoming table is one that invites all people. I believe the table is open to everyone. The last thing the world needs is more barriers to relationships, walls that increase separation, and borders that divide faith. The table is one of the few places where we are invited to bring our entire selves and to honor the fullness of those seated with us. If we believe that God's open table expands our connection with other human beings, then we are compelled to open the table up to as many people as possible and share this amazing gift. When God calls together God's beloved people, it is a place genuinely and truly open to all.

The Priestly Jesus is no more important than the other three natures of Jesus, but without it, the other three would be built on spiritual and theological ground that is at best shaky and at worst nonexistent. Without a strong foundation of inward belief, what is outwardly expressed can waver and be "tossed and blown around by every wind that comes from teaching with deceitful scheming and the tricks people play to deliberately mislead others" (Ephesians 4:14). But with the grounding of the Priestly Jesus, there is a greater chance that one lives one's faith with integrity, consistency, and confidence.

Being and Becoming Priests

For about fifteen years, I was a church planter in San Francisco. This meant that my family never really had a choice about what church they would attend, so when I left that church, my wife and I left it up to the kids to decide on our next home church. Our church-shopping process was an interesting one. As we began the process, in order to get a solid glimpse of the community, we agreed that we would attend each church at least three Sundays in a row. Because so many churches are eager for young families to attend, I can only imagine every congregation's excitement when our young family of five walked into worship multiple Sundays in a row. Alas, we had to dampen their enthusiasm by telling them that we really were church shopping. Throughout the process and with each visit, my family had some lovely conversations about what did or didn't vibe with each of us about each church's worship experience.

But we still never quite felt at home anywhere.

It is important to know that the church I had a hand in starting had a fairly casual vibe with the aesthetics made of candles, pews, couches, and café tables. The music was modern jazz, the liturgy was fluid, sermons were interactive, and technology was integrated throughout. We were unapologetically Jesus-y, young adult-centered, socially progressive, and politically leftist, and we shared in communion every Sunday. We fully knew that we would not find a community exactly like ours, so as the months went by, as one could imagine, we each had our likes and dislikes about everything. Some things we could name quite clearly, while others were more gut feelings. No one church had enough of the elements for all of us: worship style, theology, demographics, preaching, music, and general vibe. The closest was a small church that reminded us all of my home church, one that folks probably would not have guessed: an older demographic with traditional worship, but oh so lovely.

And then we stumbled into Seventh Avenue Presbyterian Church. Seventh Avenue is a church located in a small commercial neighborhood in San Francisco and is often remarked upon as a church that folks walk by all the time without noticing—but people do remember it if you mention the mural with the doves. It has a rich history of solid pastoral leadership, progressive theology, aesthetically pleasing worship space, and a congregation that is small, quirky, and made of up dedicated folks from all over the United States and Europe. Of course, we shared none of that with the kids at the time; we simply attended. As soon as they realized that this church served communion every Sunday, that was it, this was our church. At the end of every service, the congregation circles the sanctuary, and, for those who choose to receive it, we receive communion as one body seeing one another as that body. It is lovely. I am not sure I would have guessed that my kids would choose Seventh Avenue; the music and liturgy were both more classical than they were used to, but the vibe of belonging and act of communion were what really counted for them.

As we think about being and becoming priestly, we do this because Jesus has been priestly to each of us, both in his life and in the resurrection, being present and showing us healing. Of course, this ministry will look different person to person, and community to community, but the same challenge and calling remain. We must be the church in the world in compassionate and connectional ways, by building our capacity for the kind of compassion and connection that Jesus offered through his ministry of presence, healing, and ritual.

10 Ways to Become the Priest God Intends You to Be

The ultimate responsibility of our priestly presence is to give witness to communal life and connections from one generation to another, so much so that we see that we are connected to greater things than one particular place and one particular time. Here are just a few prompts of ways that might happen for you.

1. Worship: If you do not already, begin moving toward weekly communion in worship. With the world being as it is, a weekly reminder of the importance of being the body together is a grounding practice that many churches observe.

2. Worship: Reimagine how offering is taken. Rather than have it solely be about the collection of money, introduce other forms of offering, integrate movement, or create alternative practices for people to engage in the act of offering. Honestly this goes for any element of worship that makes visitors uncomfortable, practices that are no longer relevant to the current congregation, or any other worship practice that is more about maintaining the practice than about connecting to the Divine.
3. Worship: Help young people to find their worshipping life by making sure that there is a worship experience that hears, honors, supports, and practices the ways they yearn to worship. Rather than having a "Youth Sunday," move toward young people having a consistent presence in worship.
4. Worship: To enrich the experience of being worship leaders, have the community craft the prayers themselves (calls to worship, prayers of the people, etc.) in addition to reading them.
5. Develop an achievable prayer discipline. Key word: achievable. Find a prayer practice that makes sense for you: when you do it, how long, what form, etc.
6. Convene a trusted group of people to pray together in a way that is achievable and meaningful. This may be a daily group text, weekly video call, or monthly coffee, but develop some kind of communal prayer life.
7. Inspired by the Seventh Generation Principle from the Haudenosaunee (Iroquois), think about the impact of your actions upon those seven generations from now. Recall who your people were seven generations before you—who they were and what impact that has upon you today. Write a letter to each: one that shares the impact of your actions on the future and one that shares how you have been formed by generations past. This may be difficult and complicated as you unpack and imagine their realities.
8. Baptism: As a way to affirm and introduce baptism, at the next baptism, adult or infant, invite all of the children to come close so they can witness the act of baptism firsthand.

9. Communion: While this may not seem creative for some, actually use the bread and cup of the people, meaning try different elements depending on the communities you are part of or want to stand in solidarity with: injera, tortillas, bao, tea, Cheerwine, etc.
10. Rituals in context: Reflect on any rituals that your community already engages in, and explore how and why they have come to be. Develop new rituals that can be offered to a variety of groups in your community that both celebrate and comfort, such as for new drivers, recent graduates, those who adopt new names, those who suffer miscarriages, those who are moving away, etc.

For the Body, Mind, and Spirit of the Priests

A going-off-to-pray miracle worker and spiritual teacher who curates holy spaces, nurtures spiritual discipline, tends our histories, and invites us into ritual as ways to connect to God.

For Personal Reflection and Movement

- When you picture the priestly people in your life, who do you see?
- When are the times you are most connected to your priestly self?
- What barriers, obstacles, or variables hold you back from being priestly?
- Are there family or community rituals that make you feel deeply connected to past generations?
- What would an achievable weekly or monthly prayer discipline look like for you?

For Communal Reflection and Movement

- When has your community been its most priestly?
- When has your community struggled with being priestly?
- What is your community doing today to prepare for who will be the community in fifty years?

- Are there any communal rituals unique to your community?
- What communal rituals feed you the most?
- What communal rituals do you understand the least?

Prayers for the Priests

Let us pray…

One: God of the teachers, the academics,

ALL: the guides, the pray-ers,

One: those who tell us to breathe, those who bring ritual to life,

ALL: and those who sing the wisdom of the cloud of witness and ancestors of faith into God's hopes for us today, we come to you in prayer.

One: In a world that chooses immediacy over deliberation,

ALL: God, hear our prayer.

One: Allow us each the discipline to take the time to access the priestly practices that will more deeply connect us to You.

ALL: God, hear our prayer.

One: If there are ways that our community may make better Your connections, teachings, disciplines, and rituals, grant us courage and clarity to change.

ALL: God, hear our prayer.

One: In a world where speed and productivity are valued over all else, may we be a place that witnesses to the world the power and importance of being grounded, staying connected, and slowing down.

ALL: God, hear our prayer.

One: God, whether the priestly voices ring from inside or outside of this community,

ALL: grant us courage to hear. Amen.

The Pastoral Jesus

Peace I leave with you. My peace I give you. —*John 14:27*

12 Ways to Know You Might Vibe with the Pastoral Jesus

- Your soul sings when a group of people take time to work through conflict and eventually finds consensus on a path forward.
- You naturally excel at creating spaces where people feel welcomed.
- You nerd out about party planning.
- You are always prepared with a good get-to-know-you question.
- An ideal retreat would be one where you get to know people as humans.
- You never pass up a chance to engage in conversation to get to know someone more deeply.
- It bothers you when people believe that seeing the "enemy" as human is a weakness.
- In your bag right now, you have an invitation for someone to join your family for a holiday dinner if they have nowhere to go.
- Others affirm your ability to bring diverse types of people together across beliefs, life experiences, personalities, etc.

- You are often misunderstood as too trusting and too willing to give others the benefit of the doubt.
- One thing you want people to remember is that we do not get to choose who is or is not part of the body of Christ or the body politic, so when one part suffers, we all suffer.
- Your greatest hope for the church is that we will find ways to continue to be one of the places in the world where folks from diverse walks of life unexpectedly find themselves gathered in space.

Jesus as Pastor

A "giving the benefit of the doubt" convenor of relationships, instigator of belonging, and unapologetic bridge builder who yearns for us to cross cultural, economic, and theological divides as a way to know the expansiveness of God's created.

The Pastoral Jesus

Whenever people ask me about my vision of the church, I have always lifted up the image of the 2001 animated classic *Rudolph the Red-Nosed Reindeer and the Island of Misfit Toys,* which was based off of the 1964 version of *Rudolph the Red-Nosed Reindeer.* The Island of Misfit Toys was the place where all the toys that had something just a little off about them went to live. Rudolph, himself a misfit because of his red nose, found camaraderie with a train with square wheels, a squirt gun that shot jelly, a rocking horse unable to rock, a doll with clinical depression and low self-esteem, and many more.

While the world might label this a group of weirdos and outcasts, I think this is church at its best. And—I say this in the most affectionate way possible—the church should be a place where misfits belong. It's a place for those who don't belong anywhere else, where belonging is not based on appearance or abilities or fiscal situations. It's not a place of conformity or homogeneity. What makes you a little different? What makes you a little prickly? What quirk gives you character? Bring it all. Ideally, church lets us all bring our full selves. There are very few places where such a group of misfits could gather. In church we gather around this irrational belief that Someone in the universe is calling us to be different—and not just different alone, but different together. Someone has called us into this space and invited us to be fully who we are, with our pains and our sorrows, our hopes and our glee. Unlike anywhere else in the world, we can bring our full selves into this space. Do we always get it right? Of course not. Is it always rainbows and unicorns? Definitely not. But no matter what the seasons, rhythms, ebbs, and flows of life, it is usually a vision of the "kin-dom" of God that says belonging is for everyone.

The Pastoral Jesus is the one who thrives and finds meaning in creating, convening, and curating these kinds of spaces, spaces marked by compassion, empathy, and grace, that ensure that people feel seen, known, and valued. These spaces do not measure inclusion based on belief, status, or experience, but rather by a willingness to be open to the possibilities that community in Christ may offer. It is exactly this kind of profound recognition and belonging that Christian community is called to emulate: a radical inclusion that is not conditional on appearance, status, or any human category—you see, my Island of Misfit Toys.

How Jesus Shows Up as a Pastor

The Pastoral Jesus takes many forms: healer, guide, comforter, encourager, and more. The overarching theme of the Pastoral Jesus is presence and belonging. Jesus shows up, and he shows up for everyone—sinner, saint, friend, or foe—to send the message you are seen, you are known, and no matter what the world may tell you, you belong.

The Pastoral Jesus offers presence and belonging to the disciples over and over again, giving their spirits peace.

- In John 14:27, the disciples are becoming anxious about what it means to follow Jesus, and he eases their spirits by saying to them, "Peace I leave with you. My peace I give you."
- In Mark 4:37–38, Jesus was on a boat with the disciples when they became terrified in the midst of a storm. "He got up and

gave orders to the wind, and he said to the lake, 'Silence! Be still!' The wind settled down and there was a great calm" (v. 39).

- When the disciples were feeling lost or confused to the point of not even recognizing Jesus, like when they were cowering in the locked room after he was crucified, he appeared out of nowhere to bring calm. "Jesus came and stood among them. He said, 'Peace be with you.' After he said this, he showed them his hands and his side. When the disciples saw the Lord, they were filled with joy" (John 20:19–20).
- On the road to Emmaus, just after the disciples learned that Jesus was resurrected, they were traveling and trying to process all that had happened. Jesus came and walked with them, but they didn't recognize him until "he took his seat at the table with them, he took the bread, blessed and broke it, and gave it to them. Their eyes were opened and they recognized him, but he disappeared from their sight" (Luke 24:30–31).
- And in Matthew 14:22–33, when they were scared by yet another storm, he showed up walking on the water and further terrified them because they thought he was a ghost. At that moment he just told them, "Be encouraged! It's me. Don't be afraid" (v. 27)—and then invited them into the same miraculous experience as himself, which Peter, of course, immediately accepted!

Sometimes, when examined through the eyes of today's world, the messages of Jesus are painfully obvious. So it is no surprise the OG disciples didn't always get it the first time. Jesus knew this, so with love and compassion, he reminded them as often as needed that they were not alone.

Jesus was present with the disciples; he also extended a ministry of presence and belonging to those he met throughout his ministry. More than healing, casting out demons, and raising people from the dead, through his ministry he offered gestures of presence and belonging to individuals and communities.

In Matthew 14, he fed lots of people, five to ten thousand counting everyone, even when the disciples didn't believe it was possible. "But

Jesus said to them, 'There's no need to send them away. You give them something to eat'" (v. 16).

In Matthew 5, he shares the Beatitudes or eight blessings in his Sermon on the Mount: "Now when Jesus saw the crowds, he went up a mountain. He sat down and his disciples came to him. He taught them" (vv. 1–2).

He often made people feel seen, as in Mark 7:26–30 when he acknowledged the Syrophoenician woman's humanity and her daughter's hurt after initially buying into the cultural prejudice of the time. "The woman was Greek, Syrophoenician by birth. She begged Jesus to throw the demon out of her daughter. He responded, 'The children have to be fed first. It isn't right to take the children's bread and toss it to the dogs.' But she answered, 'Lord, even the dogs under the table eat the children's crumbs.' 'Good answer!' he said. 'Go on home. The demon has already left your daughter.' When she returned to her house, she found the child lying on the bed and the demon gone."

Pretty much any interaction in which Jesus saw someone who was not seen by everyone else became an act of pastoral presence and an invitation to belonging. When people are in pain, in need of healing, and the world denies them relief, Jesus simply heals.

- Jesus heals the woman who touches the hem of his cloak in Mark 5:34: "Daughter, your faith has healed you; go in peace, healed from your disease."
- He heals the leper in Luke 5:13: "Jesus reached out his hand, touched him, and said, 'I do want to. Be clean.' Instantly, the skin disease left him,"
- He heals the paralytic in Mark 2:10–12: "'But so you will know that the Human One has authority on the earth to forgive sins'—he said to the man who was paralyzed, 'Get up, take your mat, and go home.' Jesus raised him up, and right away he picked up his mat and walked out in front of everybody."

The list goes on and on. Jesus heals not only the body, but the heart and soul. And in doing so, he helps people to remember that through these interactions there is hope, and hope in the One called Christ.

Whether an act of presence, invitation, or healing, the important thing to note about Jesus' pastoral interactions is that they always help people to connect with others, not only with Jesus himself. The ultimate example of showing up and invitation takes place on Easter Sunday morning.

In Mark 16:9–11, Jesus shows up after Mary discovered that Jesus was resurrected. "After Jesus rose up early on the first day of the week, he appeared first to Mary Magdalene, from whom he had cast out seven demons. She went and reported to the ones who had been with him, who were mourning and weeping. But even after they heard the news, they didn't believe that Jesus was alive and that Mary had seen him."

He also shows up in John 20:16–18 when Mary goes to the tomb and is confused about where Jesus is. "Jesus said to her, 'Mary.' She turned and said to him in Aramaic, 'Rabbouni' (which means Teacher). Jesus said to her, 'Don't hold on to me, for I haven't yet gone up to my Father. Go to my brothers and sisters and tell them, "I'm going up to my Father and your Father, to my God and your God."' Mary Magdalene left and announced to the disciples, 'I've seen the Lord.' Then she told them what he said to her."

From the first telling of the resurrection through growing numbers of people who come to believe in it over time, we are reminded that we are part of the body of Christ and the body politic. This is not only a gift to respond to but a privilege to bear. To be part of this body, we are held up by others when we do not have the strength to do it ourselves, and we do the same for others when they in turn are in need. The resurrection is the ultimate symbol of God saying that not only do you belong to one another in this life, but in life and in death, you belong to me.

How Pastors Show Up in the World

A few years back, I was speaking at church and was introduced by someone I didn't know very well. I have a standard introduction that is used, but they went off script and said, "Bruce is a convener of people." In all honesty, I had not felt so seen in a very long time. And yes, that has been in some form in my social media bios ever since.

The reason I deeply appreciated someone naming that part of my journey is that it acknowledged a part of my call that I have always held in very high regard. Gathering people together to create a situation where belonging is a possibility is a deliberate process. There have been times when I have believed in the "pied piper" style of leadership where one just has to be charismatic or able to perform a party trick or two. But I have learned that over time, that draw loses steam because it is built upon only the traits of one person. We have seen this time and time again, and not just in churches: a cult of personality may be successful and even feel good to folks, right up until that particular personality can no longer maintain the same level of expectation or energy. Then people drift away because the belonging was not to a community, but to a personality. They may have been given worth, but it was meted out by one source, and as soon as that source was gone or changed, the worthiness disappeared with it.

The Pastoral Jesus recognized that to offer belonging was to offer personal connection and presence that guided people toward becoming community.

Curating space where people feel like they belong means creating a space where disagreement can happen in healthy and agreed upon ways. Too often, especially in today's political climate, people say that all we need to do to solve our problems is talk with one another. Oh, if it were only that simple. I do not disagree that more dialogue would be helpful, but just putting people in a room without understanding expectations, boundaries, etc, for a conversational free-for-all is dangerous—emotionally, spiritually, and sadly even physically. Curating spaces for conversations where there may be conflict takes work to give those conversations a chance at a positive outcome. Not all people are equipped for this work, but those called to create these kinds of interactions have a pastoral heart.

Being and Becoming Pastors

I really am obsessed with the Island of Misfit Toys metaphor that I used when introducing the Pastoral Jesus earlier in this chapter. And I must confess, when I walk into a church and everyone looks the same or there is a homogeneity vibe going on, I get a little judgy. I am not saying it's right, just being honest. I realize that is more about the particular communities that I feel called to pastor and not about those that I judge to be all the same. I must remember that even the most outwardly homogenous community has a diversity of struggles and issues going on in the background and deserves pastoral spaces as much as anyone else. No matter what your community looks like, it should strive to be like the Island of Misfit Toys, where everyone has the chance to experience belonging.

Please note that you cannot force someone to experience belonging, there is no recipe to create belonging, and there is no guarantee that one community can create belonging for all people. Belonging is a secret sauce, that family ingredient that Grandpa will never share, or that feeling you just get when you walk into a space. Belonging is something for which you create space, then cultivate its growth when and if it happens.

One of the ways that we can best create belonging today as individuals and congregations is to be the *third place* of people's lives. Third places are gathering places outside of work and family where community happens and where people can deepen relationships. The draws are different, but the results are the same, belonging and creating spaces of impact on the individual and the world.

According to Ray Oldenburg, author of *The Great Good Place,* when he discusses the nature of "regulars" in "third places" he describes them as devoid of the "blandness of strangers" option for a more connected and unique relationship that he calls the "commended stranger." A space filled with strangers who are connected by a common draw creates a dynamic that "breathes life into our conversation." Yes, "the church" has a great deal to lament, confess, and atone for. In another instance of "many things can be true at the same time," the church is also a place where people experience healing and wholeness. As we think about creating spaces of belonging, we must be mindful not to allow our spaces to become spaces of exclusion. We all have tendencies to turn inward as community is built and strengthened. It becomes more and more difficult to let new people into the stronger community that grows. This happens because we trick ourselves into thinking that the community grows stronger by not letting new people in, when in fact a community grows stronger precisely because new people become part of it. Just as new germs help to build stronger immunity in physical bodies over time, new ideas build stronger cultures in the body politic in the same way. We have to fight the urge to turn inward and protect what is ours as our first and only instinct, instead being open to others' ideas for building communities of belonging, even when growing pains accompany them.

The ultimate role of pastoral people is to remind one another that we are not alone on this journey. We belong to God, so we belong to one another. When one part of the body suffers, the entire body suffers. And when one part of the body rejoices, the entire body rejoices. We are reminded that we need one another for the long journey of faith, that we will not survive without one another, and that the journey itself will be less full without all of us traveling it together.

10 Ways to Become the Pastor God Intends You to Be

Being pastoral requires a deep well of awareness of context, content, and culture. How actions are perceived or derived will vary depending on what people have experienced in their personal or faith lives. It would be wonderful if most people have had positive experiences with church and religion, but as we know, this is not the case. Because of this, we must be careful not to treat my suggestions as rigid tactics to implement with expected outcomes. Instead, these practices must be translated and adapted to meet the needs of your particular context.

1. Check for consistency between what you say about belonging and how you live it out. In other words, reflect upon how well you practice what you preach, and explore putting action behind your words. For example, if you say in your worship service, "Visit the imprisoned," but no one in your congregation has visited a jail, detention center, or prison in recent memory,

this is a great opportunity to talk about how you are or are not "present" and how you might become more so.

2. Assess how welcoming you are. This could be done by talking with visitors who have not returned (if you can contact them), relatives who have visited, or others you know who have visited and can offer feedback.
3. Offer your facilities as a third place for community events so folks can become comfortable and familiar with the space itself: candidate forums, town hall meetings, author talks, community trainings, etc.
4. Have a presence at local events to show that you are connected to and interested in being part of the community outside of the church walls: night markets, Pride events, etc.
5. Create focused seasonal or topical small groups: Be it a book group or a tough topic discussion group, they should be time bound and could be a way for folks across generations to connect.
6. Create a culture and practice of life stage small groups. Talk to most churches, especially ones that are growing or have long-term members, and their small groups will often come up as their community anchor. Long-term small groups are best done by life stage so they can mature and navigate life stages together.

(These last four are examples that I believe create excellent opportunities for people to experience belonging. It is obviously not exhaustive and must be paired with number 1, consistency of words and deeds.)

7. Prison ministry: Connect with organizations that serve people who are incarcerated. This could be visiting jails or prisons, but it could also be finding ways for people to stay connected with family and community.
8. College ministry: Invest time, energy, and resources to this age group—not in order for the church to survive, but to provide

stability, community, and an occasional homecooked meal to young adults during a season of life that can be isolating.

9. Camp and conference ministry: In a world filled with constant stimulation, camps and conferences can provide moments of respite, retreat, and re-creation.
10. Solidarity vigils: Too often churches are absent from the public square concerning issues of injustice. During times of crisis, take part in organizing and hosting vigils when the larger community needs to experience belonging.

For the Body, Mind, and Spirit of the Pastors

A "giving the benefit of the doubt" convenor of relationships, instigator of belonging, and unapologetic bridge builder who yearns for us to cross cultural, economic, and theological divides as a way to know the expansiveness of God's created.

For Personal Reflection and Movement

- When you picture the pastoral people in your life, who do you see?
- When was a time you felt deeply pastoral?
- What barriers, obstacles, or variables hold you back from being pastoral?
- Where have you found the place of deepest belonging, and why do you think that was so?
- Is there anyone specific you know in need of a place of belonging, and how might you be part of making that happen?

For Communal Reflection and Movement

- What does belonging look or feel like in your community?
- When has your community struggled with being pastoral?
- What are the "third places" in your community, and what do they offer?

- What are the top three or four reasons people say they feel like they "belong" in your community?
- Who might feel like they do *not* "belong," and why?

Prayers for the Pastors

Let us pray…

One: God of the gatherers, the organizers,

ALL: the healers, and the aisle crossers,

One: for those who welcome the weird, those who convene spaces of welcome and belonging,

ALL: and those who lead with empathy, kindness, and the benefit of the doubt for all of God's creation, we come to you in prayer.

One: In a world that chooses to see the health of the individual as separate from health of the whole,

ALL: God, hear our prayer.

One: Allow us each empathy enough to act in a way with others that embodies the presence, love, and healing of Jesus.

ALL: God, hear our prayer.

One: If there are ways that our community may better express Your belonging, grant us courage and wisdom to change.

ALL: God, hear our prayer.

One: In a world that deals in suspicion, judgment, and exclusivity, may we be a place where misfits, weirdos, and the "othered" find a place of genuine belonging.

ALL: God, hear our prayer.

One: God, whether the pastoral voices ring out from inside or outside of this community,

ALL: grant us courage to hear. Amen.

The Poetic Jesus

Jesus said to her, "Mary."—John 20:16

12 Ways to Know You Might Vibe with the Poetic Jesus

- Your soul sings when people are faced with new ideas and their first reaction is to open themselves up to what may be.
- You naturally excel at crafting words and images to help people expand their vision and understanding of the world.
- You nerd out about helping people to experience classic things in modern ways.
- You are always prepared to tell a good story.
- An ideal retreat would be to examine and reimagine every element of a worship service: the purpose, the liturgy, and the vibe.
- You never pass up a chance to experience something new.
- It bothers you when people view being creative as an activity to undertake only if time permits, after the "real" work is done.
- In your bag right now you have a sketchpad, a book of poetry, a long list of "when I have time" projects, or a list of creatives you need to check out.

- Others affirm your ability to come up with creative solutions.
- You are often misunderstood as unrealistic, naive, or unserious.
- You want people to remember that creativity doesn't only show up in people who are "artistic" but is expressed in all ways that humans live and move through the world.
- Your greatest hope for the church is that it understands the unbelievability of the resurrection not as a convenient idea, but as a foregone promise.

Jesus as Poet

A "more questions than answers" sculptor of words, ideas, and actions and one who pries open the human imagination in order to see the possibilities that God has for the world.

The Poetic Jesus

As noted at the beginning of this book, the world is in a troubled place. As I was writing this book, I dined with a friend I have known for decades. Our kids are the same age, we have a similar worldview, and we have worked together on issues of social justice. At one point during our conversation, they paused and asked me, "Bruce, are you still hopeful?"

The way they looked at me, I could tell that they were not. They went on to share how they had simply lost hope in the world. They had been working their entire life to change the world for the better, doing the right things, making hopeful choices in work and life, and motivating others to engage in the work of positive change. And now they felt it was all for naught. The environmental damage has passed the point of no return, a small percentage of oligarchs are now driving decisions that impact a greater majority of people than ever, and our political system is breaking down before our very eyes. At the end of the conversation they said, "I have given up all hope."

All I could do at that moment was simply be present. That was not the time for me to share that I was still foolish enough to be hopeful. Now do not get me wrong, I would be ecstatic if, by the time you are reading this book, the world has been healed and all is well—but I will not hold my breath. As people have been at any point in history, I am sure we are not alone in looking around at all of the hatred, destruction, and sorrow of the world and feeling overwhelmed by the sense that there is no way things will ever get better. To be honest, I sit in that space often, that place where my faith suffers from a lack of imagination and I cannot get beyond what my head and heart can imagine right there and then. And while I believe humans are lovely and generally good, without outside help, I am not confident that we humans on our own can get out of the destruction and terror we have created.

This is why for me, at the heart of my faith, the most important aspect of Jesus is the poetic one. This part of Jesus reminds us that God's intentions for humanity lie far beyond our imagination. The Poetic Jesus inspires imagination, creativity, and openness to the miraculous possibilities that God may reveal before us. This is made known through miracles, parables, and the capacity for Jesus to challenge us to reinterpret the realities in which we may be confined.

The Poetic Jesus steps into the world in a variety of ways, even expanding the very idea of creativity itself. The Poetic Jesus is the one who forces us to remain open to the unfolding of God's intentions in all aspects of our communal life—worship, social interactions, and organizational structures—so we can experience the expansiveness that God hopes for us all. And at the end of the day, Jesus drops the ultimate poem before us. This poem reminds us that, despite the despair, sorrow, and suffering surrounding us, in the unimaginable act of resurrection there is always hope.

How Jesus Shows Up as a Poet

Throughout scripture Jesus shows us how to reimagine the world beyond the confines and limitations of what the world's imagination allows itself.

When Jesus shows up in the locked room after the disciples ran away to hide because they were overwhelmed by what had happened to Jesus, it is a little like how many of us, including my friend, are feeling—as if the world is closing in around us. In response, many of us, like the disciples, have built a wall around what was possible, locking out the possibilities that Jesus promised: in three days, he would come back. They needed a miracle to remind them of the promise of hope. Yet even when Jesus showed up, they could not fathom the possibility that it was him until he assured them: "He said, 'Peace be with you.' After he said this, he showed them his hands and his side. When the disciples saw the Lord, they were filled with joy" (John 20:19–20). Only then did the walls of their imaginations come tumbling down and the possibilities become real.

While it would be much more helpful if Jesus simply showed up and told us slowly and clearly, IT WILL BE OKAY, his assurances often require some work on our part. We must always be open to the possibilities because Jesus the Poet shows up throughout scripture every time he feeds, heals, or does anything that pushes people outside of what they could imagine. Every miracle, every parabolic takedown, every instance of tearing down some confining wall of the spirit is a poetic act.

Jesus' challenge is to think beyond what the world would want us to think with every miracle.

- In Matthew 19:21, Jesus tells the rich young man who had followed all the commandments he thought he was supposed to in order to please God, "If you want to be complete, go, sell what you own, and give the money to the poor. Then you will have treasure in heaven. And come follow me." In this act, Jesus lifted the limitations of what the man thought was going to be asked of him—and the man discovered that he was not willing or able to live with that expansive of a commitment. In the end, he could not embrace the miracle Jesus offered.
- Jesus brought sight to a man blind since birth. As told by the man in John 9:11, "The man they call Jesus made mud, smeared it on my eyes, and said, 'Go to the pool of Siloam and wash.' So I went and washed, and then I could see."

- Jesus calms storms in Mark 4:39: "He got up and gave orders to the wind, and he said to the lake, 'Silence! Be still!' The wind settled down and there was a great calm."
- He feeds people from scraps in Matthew 15:37–38: "Everyone ate until they were full. The disciples collected seven baskets full of leftovers. Four thousand men ate, plus women and children."
- He casts out demons in Luke 4:40–41: "Placing his hands on each of them, he healed them. Demons also came out of many people."
- He cures lifelong afflictions like in Luke 13:12–13, when a woman was weighed down by physical and cultural burdens: "When he saw her, Jesus called her to him and said, 'Woman, you are set free from your sickness.' He placed his hands on her and she straightened up at once and praised God."
- He walks on water in Matthew 14:25 to show what is possible when there is faith: "Very early in the morning he came to his disciples, walking on the lake."
- He turns water into wine in John 2:7–9 at the great wedding banquet to show the power of transformation and abundance: "Jesus said to the servants, 'Fill the jars with water,' and they filled them to the brim. Then he told them, 'Now draw some from them and take it to the headwaiter,' and they did. The headwaiter tasted the water that had become wine."
- And, oh yeah, he raises people from the dead, like in Luke 7:14–15 when he raised the widow's son: "He stepped forward and touched the stretcher on which the dead man was being carried. Those carrying him stood still. Jesus said, 'Young man, I say to you, get up.' The dead man sat up and began to speak, and Jesus gave him to his mother."

Miracles all. In each case, what was thought to be impossible became real: poetry to the extreme.

And what about those parables? To borrow a term from the young people: the Poetic Jesus was the GOAT at getting his point across through the use of metaphor, whether it was a feeding, a transformation, a rebuke, a healing, or a rebuttal for those trying to back him into a theological corner, Jesus' metaphorical storytelling through the use of parables. Parables by their very nature are meant to stretch our thinking. Parables, then as today, sometimes confuse and confound and other times open up new ways of seeing the world and the expansiveness of God.

There are many parables that illustrate Jesus challenging people to think beyond the easy answer, which means that there are many interpretations. Here are a few.

- The parable of the talents can be interpreted to critique capitalism and greed: "The kingdom of heaven is like a man who was leaving on a trip. He called his servants and handed his possessions over to them. To one he gave five valuable coins, and to another he gave two, and to another he gave one. He gave to each servant according to that servant's ability. Then he left on his journey" (Matthew 25:14–15).
- There was also the parable of the sower demonstrating the ways God's love is generously shared and how it may be heard: "A farmer went out to scatter his seed" (Luke 8:5).
- And the parable of new wineskins challenges us to look at radical change: "Then he told them a parable. 'No one tears a patch from a new garment to patch an old garment. Otherwise, the new garment would be ruined, and the new patch wouldn't match the old garment. Nobody pours new wine into old wineskins. If they did, the new wine would burst the wineskins, the wine would spill, and the wineskins would be ruined. Instead, new wine must be put into new wineskins. No one who drinks a well-aged wine wants new wine, but says, "The well-aged wine is better"'" (Luke 5:36–39).

Each of these challenges the hearer to think for themselves and interpret what the story might mean. Jesus offers some help, but at the end of the day, he is loosing us from the confines of what is holding us back from more fully experiencing God's movement in our lives. The parables give us permission to break free.

Lastly, one of the most beautiful images of the Poetic Jesus comes from Mark 7 when he responds to the Syrophoenician woman asking for healing for her daughter. His initial response was to fling pejoratives based on her low status. She ends up tearing down the walls that even Jesus had, so much so that he changes his perspective and heals the child: "But she answered, 'Lord, even the dogs under the table eat the children's crumbs.' 'Good answer!' he said. 'Go on home. The demon has already left your daughter'" (vv. 28–29). In this, the humanity of Jesus shows through and demonstrates that he too can be stretched and changed. Some Christians have a difficult time seeing Jesus as being a person of his day, racist and misogynistic, but I love seeing the fully human part of Jesus in full display. If Jesus can see beyond the barriers and bounds of his time, how dare we not be open to doing the same?

These miracles, parables, and transformations are here not simply to show us how fabulous Jesus was. He was not showing off. Everything he did was proof and preparation for the ultimate miracle of the Poetic Jesus and the ultimate poem of God, the resurrection of Christ Jesus and the opportunity to believe in something unbelievable. The uniqueness of our Christian faith is that we have the audacity and confidence to believe in a God who can and will do things in the world that we cannot even begin to imagine. And while each person needs to arrive at their own understanding of the resurrection, for me, few things are more unimaginable, audacious, and outrageous than a human, fflesh-and-blood person coming back from the dead. It is understandably difficult to imagine that this act is what gives our faith meaning.

How Poets Show Up in the World

How many times have you imitated your favorite sports hero and heard the play-by-play in your head? *The ball is hit up the middle for a single. Unbelievable—Reyes-Chow just dove to his left and somehow got to that ball. He pops up and throws out the fastest runner to ever play the game of baseball to win game seven of the World Series! Holy Toledo, the crowd goes wild!"* Oh wait, just me?

I am sure it is not just me. Surely, someone reading this book has watched themselves hold their own while belting a tune on stage with Beyoncé, stood back in wonder after performing a magic trick that would have confounded Houdini himself, or told a story so profound that there was not a dry eye in the house from crying (or a gut not sore from laughing). If you are like me, whenever you see someone make an amazing feat look easy, a small part of you gets inspired and thinks, *I can do that.* When I see amazing artists or thinkers, they inspire me to strive to do the same thing they are sharing with the world. This is not because I actually believe I can do all of these things. I am mostly a rational adult human and know my limitations. But the poets of the world inspire us, even for a moment, to think beyond rationality and believe that we can, in fact, do great things. It does not last long, but we are given a glimpse into what it means to believe in something greater than what the world wants us to believe.

As we think about the poets of the world, it is important not to fall into the trap of believing that the Poetic Jesus is a solo act and we are simply an audience waiting for the miracle to happen. Miracles can take time to manifest and often need many of us to participate in their expression. The miracle of the Poetic Jesus can last more than a moment, more than a generation, if only we would cultivate the spiritual soil for that belief to flourish. In the Poetic Jesus, we are reminded that the work and ministry of the church and community can create options to a world of despair, destruction, sorrow, and hate.

Being and Becoming Poets

Planning for a conference, I invited a friend, Rev. Shawna Bowman, to help facilitate a portion of the gathering by helping with creativity and artistry in worship. As we were planning the schedule, I laid out my idea for the flow of the days: planning, preaching, music/liturgy, art/creativity. After a moment, they responded by basically pushing back on the fact that creativity in worship is too often an afterthought. Thinking creatively is often brought up if there is enough time, when it should be the first question, the lens through which everything else should be planned. Creativity should not be treated as just window dressing, swirling fabric, and making things vibe—though the vibe is extremely important—but as an invitation to the Spirit to guide all aspects of the service. So we moved the element "creativity" to the front of the event, and it was liberating for us all.

What Shawna reminded me was that to be creative and imaginative is not only about being artistic. It certainly *can* be. Shawna is an amazing fine artist. On multiple occasions, Shawna has created art while I was preaching. (One guess which activity people were more excited about.) In addition, they are extremely creative in thinking about building community and organizing movements, as evident in their call as pastor and executive director of Friendship Presbyterian Church and Friendship Community Place in northwest Chicago.

To be poetic and creative, our imaginations can and must be manifested in a multitude of ways in our lives. In our institutions and organizations, we must be creative about structures that help us move closer to who and how God hopes us to be. In our communities, we must constantly reflect on cultural norms to make sure we are not limiting the ways in which we may feel included or include others. The same can be said for political movements, faith communities, educational institutions, social environments, and anywhere else we may find ourselves getting caught up in narrow ways of thinking.

While being creative and accessing the depth of our imagination may feel daunting, it offers us possibilities beyond what we can imagine. That is the very miracle of the Poetic Jesus. Jesus, the Poet, prods and pushes us out of our spaces of comfort. The Poet Jesus reminds us that the possibility of hope is not out of reach. And through it all, Jesus reinforces for us, as he did with the confused, hurt, and weary disciples, that healing, abundance, and hope await on the other side of the struggle.

10 Ways to Become the Poet God Intends You to Be

As I have mentioned, it is important not to think about the Poetic Christ and the possibilities he may reveal as solely within the confines of what we understand as traditional "artistry" (e.g., performing or fine arts). For this reason, in this section I have been specific in breaking down the ten examples into distinct areas of ministry and faith.

1. Worship: Play with the format of the proclamation moment by trying different forms of storytelling: crowd-work style, conversational, small groups, multi-person spoken word, etc. Introduce these ideas during a liturgical season, giving people permission to play and experience without the pressure of permanence.
2. Worship: Change settings and perspectives by either rearranging current space as much as possible or holding worship in a completely different venue and integrating that new space's elements into the flow and vibe of the service.
3. Worship: Engage in a process of evaluating and reimagining your current services. Have folks worship somewhere else on a particular Sunday, at as many diverse types of churches as possible. Afterward, share what was learned and how that might impact what worship could look like at your church in the future.
4. Worship: Find ways to integrate all senses into the worship experience: touch, sound, sight, and yes, smell and taste.
5. Organization: Undergo a process of reflecting upon the mission and vision of the church by inventorying all programs and activities of the church, staff and volunteer energy, and financial resources to see whether they align with the mission and vision. If they do not, dream of possible ways to better use those resources so they do.
6. Digital: Engage in a full internet and website audit with the goal to create a digital footprint that creatively and truthfully tells the story of who you are now and who you hope to become as a community. Find out for whom this kind of task is exciting and who has demonstrated experience and then invite them in.
7. Arts: Find a blank wall on your property and develop a plan to create a communal mural. Partner with a local mural group

to help the community develop a design and create the mural itself.

8. Arts: Create art for the worship space that will not be saved. Think through a process of crafting and creating something for a particular liturgical season that will only be in existence for that one season. In thinking about a piece as a one-off, the community can release many questions that come with permanency and free up energy to dream.
9. Community: Hold a brainstorming time when the church gathers to dream about what God may be revealing for them in the future, what their deepest yearnings are for the church, and what they would love to be part of co-creating with God. Stay away from drifting into "why we can't" but use it as a first step toward concrete action.
10. Community: Hold a talent-sharing weekend where people sign up to teach a class on something to which they bring experience. This lets people share their passions, deepens communal relationships, and gives people a chance to try on a new thought or practice. For example, "Weightlifting with Abby" or "Baking with Ev" or "Roller Derby with Annie." Structure it so people can take multiple classes in a day, and have the registration fees go to a local organization.

For the Body, Mind, and Spirit of the Poets

A "more questions than answers" sculptor of words, ideas, and actions and one who pries open the human imagination in order to see the possibilities that God has for the world.

For Personal Reflection and Movement

- When you picture the poetic people in your life, who do you see?
- When was a time when you were undeniably poetic?
- What barriers, obstacles, or variables hold you back from being poetic?

- What activity have you always wanted to try but may have thought it not possible?
- What is one place, issue, or situation where you most hope to expand your imagination for what is possible?

For Communal Reflection and Movement

- When has your community been its most poetic?
- When has your community struggled with being poetic?
- Are there ways your community has been creative, imaginative, or "out of the box" that have nothing to do with what would be considered "artistic"?
- What are the most significant obstacles to the community accessing the depth of its imagination?
- What dreams do you have for your community?

Prayers for the Poets

Let us pray…

One: God of the artists, the non-anxious,

ALL: the curious, the creatives,

One: those who think expansively about all things, those who open up our senses to divine awe and wonder,

ALL: and those who inspire us to believe, really believe, that all things are possible in God, we come to you in prayer.

One: In a world that chooses what is known over what could be,

ALL: God, hear our prayer.

One: Allow us each faith enough to choose discomfort and vulnerability to risk venturing into unknown spaces.

ALL: God, hear our prayer.

One: If there are ways that our community has become walled

off from Your possibilities in our culture, systems, or theology, grant us the courage and curiosity to change.

ALL: God, hear our prayer.

One: In a world where speed and productivity are valued over all else, may we be a place that witnesses to the world the power and importance of being grounded, staying connected, and slowing down.

ALL: God, hear our prayer.

One: God, whether the poetic voices ring from inside or outside of this community,

ALL: grant us courage to hear. Amen.

As You Go

"Jesus came near and spoke to them, 'I've received all authority in heaven and on earth. Therefore, go and make disciples of all nations, baptizing them in the name of the Father and of the Son and of the Holy Spirit, teaching them to obey everything that I've commanded you. Look, I myself will be with you every day until the end of this present age'" (Matthew 28:18–20).

One of the most challenging aspects of Jesus for many people is the fear that talking about Jesus automatically places a person into the same category as "dude standing on the corner dressed in a sandwich board and a megaphone, damning people to hell because they have not accepted Jesus Christ as their Lord and Savior."

And while that is certainly one way to share Jesus (to be perfectly clear, a way that I believe does more damage than good), there is a lot of space between shouting on the street corner and doing absolutely nothing to share how your belief in Jesus Christ guides your life. After all, our faith must not be one that we keep to ourselves, only for private consumption and personal gain. Our faith demands us to express what we believe out loud—especially in a day and age when there is version of the gospel flooding the cultural airwaves characterizing a Christian faith that reinforces exclusion, division, and violence. How dare we not be equally as vocal and present with a faith built upon extending hospitality, seeking the common good, and striving for wholeness?

When it comes to "sharing the gospel," there are a couple of ways to think about this. We could spend a ton of energy trying to take on people with whom we disagree, those putting out a version of the gospel that runs diametrically opposed to what you or I may believe to be true. Sure, there is a time and place for that, and we should always be crystal clear that we oppose, reject, and repudiate the versions of Christianity that deserve such a reaction and spend some energy letting folks know that many Christians reject this version of the faith. But I think our time is better spent living and breathing a better version of the gospel, one that manifests compassion, love, and hope, not cruelty, hatred, and despair.

So this is my call to be "evangelists." Calm down, this wasn't a bait-and-switch. You are not being catfished, and I am not recruiting you into some conservative evangelical Christian cult. I actually do not have much use for the word "evangelist" nor any interest in reclaiming the word from those who've used it to inflict harm, violence, and the destruction of cultures and communities over the centuries. Instead, I recognize the pain and damage that have been inflicted in the name of evangelism while still believing that evangelism, at its core and as a theological concept, isn't a bad thing.

For me, evangelism is simply faith sharing, and it is part of our tradition. Evangelism means sharing the faith I believe in. I choose to talk about my faith, and if that resonates with someone else, wonderful. I do not claim that my understanding is the only or the best way to connect with God, nor do I judge others for their paths. I am comfortable sharing what I believe, but I always invite conversation rather than conversion.

I do this for the same reason that most others engage in evangelism: because our scripture says we are supposed to. It begins with the great commission—to "go and make disciples of all nations"—and that is where the agreement ends because of how you may read the word "go." I learned to interpret the great commission not as a command—an order to "Go!"—but rather as guidance to live and share my faith as I "go" through life. So for me, evangelism belongs in the everyday, woven into my actions, words, and relationships. It's about living consistently, with integrity, being the person of faith I claim and aspire to be. It is a way of being, not a weapon of faith.

When observing how Jesus lives into this "as you go" understanding of evangelism, it is not hard to see that he embodied the prophetic, pastoral, priestly, and poetic as he moved through the world. He was what was needed, as we should be. So as I move through the world, I strive to reflect whichever aspect is needed at the moment: sometimes being prophetic, sometimes priestly, sometimes poetic or pastoral.

One of many examples of Jesus being evangelical (publicly expressing who and how God wants to us to be in the world) can be found in the story of the woman at the well in John 4. This is one of my personal formative texts, and I believe Jesus models all four elements of his character in this single narrative. For those new to the story, the woman is an outcast because of culture and social standing. Therefore, the only time that she can go to the well is during the hottest part of the day, around noon.

- In verse 7 (these quotes are taken from the NIV), "When a Samaritan woman came to draw water, Jesus said to her, 'Will you give me a drink?'" Jesus spoke to the woman (gasp). Jesus was prophetic by breaking the cultural understanding that, because she was a woman and of "ill-repute," she should be isolated. Speaking to her disrupted injustice and invited her to see that she was not defined by others.
- In verses 13–14, "Jesus answered, 'Everyone who drinks this water will be thirsty again, but whoever drinks the water I give them will never thirst. Indeed, the water I give them will become in them a spring of water welling up to eternal life.'" Jesus was priestly in revealing a spiritual promise, and he invited her into a relationship with the divine and into a journey of acceptance of faith.
- In verses 25–26, "The woman said, 'I know that Messiah' (called Christ) 'is coming. When he comes, he will explain everything to us.'" This is Jesus' example of pastoral presence. Just by being there, Jesus is pastoral, creating a space where believing could

be experienced. He invites her into a community of belonging based not on what she has or has not done, but on the faith she expresses.

- When Jesus declares, "I, the one speaking to you—I am he" (v. 26), his poetic nature show up. Jesus stretches her understanding of what could be beyond what she could imagine, even beyond what was before her very eyes.

At the end of it all, Jesus invites her to an excitement about this new connection and faith, one that compels her to share this faith. "Many of the Samaritans from that town believed in him because of the woman's testimony, 'He told me everything I ever did.' So when the Samaritans came to him, they urged him to stay with them, and he stayed two days. And because of his words many more became believers" (vv. 39–41).

In these examples and more, we see that Jesus is multifaceted in how he expresses his faith. This is not duplicitous or disingenuous; it is simply being adaptive and staying attentive to the people and context around you so you can best offer what is most needed at the time.

Wherever you may land on the "evangelism" spectrum, I hope you land somewhere and on something. There are simply too many dangerous and destructive versions of Christianity out there for us to choose indifference. Ultimately, I believe the world needs a diversity of faith leaders. We need more prophetic, pastoral, priestly, and poetic voices to help others see something beyond their imagination. To me, the story of Jesus—especially the resurrection—is proof that anything can happen, that hope and unimaginable transformation are possible. This is not just a story worth telling, but a story worth living. As I go, I am committed to living and sharing this faith, true to what I believe.

I hope you'll join me and others in this endeavor.

Love God

"You must love the Lord your God with all your heart, with all your being, and with all your mind. This is the first and greatest commandment. And the second is like it: *You must love your neighbor as you love yourself"* (Matthew 22:37–40).

One of my favorite books ever is the Little Golden Book *The Monster at the End of This Book: Starring Lovable, Furry Old Grover*. If you have never read it, I'm going to spoil it for you. Grover shows up on each page warning the reader not to turn the page because there is a monster at the end of the book. With each page, Grover pleads for the reader not to turn the next page. He nails the pages shut. He ties them down. He builds walls. Until finally we get the end and the "monster" is just Grover. Lovable, furry old Grover.

The reason I love the simplicity of this children's book is that in many ways, most things that matter are quite simple. Human adults tend to complicate most things, even God, and especially Jesus. At the end of the day, at the end of the book, we are simply being called to be with God, to follow Christ's example as closely as we can. It's that simple. We muck it all up with the reasons we can't or why it's difficult, but on occasion, when we allow ourselves to turn that last page, we meet God and it is simply lovely. It's just us and God.

This commandment is so simple.

Love God.

Love your neighbor.

The stranger.

Your friend.

Your enemy.

With all your heart, all your mind, and all your soul.

Love, just love.

As we wind down our time together, I hope that you have found some simplicity of faith in these four elements of who and how Jesus can be.

Be prophetic and declare God's hopes and intentions for humanity.

Be priestly and invite others into spiritual discipline and ritual.

Be pastoral and gather the community to create spaces of belonging.

Be poetic and help inspire people to believe that what may seem impossible is possible.

There will always be reasons not to be like Christ, to get bogged down in why we cannot disrupt the norms of the day, why we don't have time to tend to our spiritual lives, why being community takes so much work, and why dreaming is foolish, but we cannot allow ourselves to build those walls and convince ourselves to stop turning the pages on our faith.

God's intentions are always for us to continue to grow, to continue to discover God's hopes, and to join in on the revealing of God's plan for humanity. There will be seasons when it feels tender and tiresome, but when we persevere and move forward as we can, what we see on the other side is often more than we could ever have imagined. That is what it means to simply love God, to keep trusting, and to keep moving.

This faith is not a passive activity, but an active adventure. Traveling the road together, and doing so with the breadth and depth that Jesus offers us, makes the journey that much more textured and life-giving.

Your Charge and Benediction

I have used the following charge and benediction at the end of every service that I have led over the past three decades of church leadership. It is an amalgamation of words gathered from various writings over the years; I'm not even sure from where they have all come, but I'm thankful for all the pieces and tidbits that have been gifted to me and have been, in turn, passed down to countless others. It always seems to be the last line that resonates with people the most, probably because it is so true.

> Let us pray:
>
> Go forth into the world with compassion and justice in your heart.
>
> Hear voices of the long-silenced.
>
> See strength in that which has been deemed weak.
>
> See one another.
>
> Hear one another.
>
> Care for one another.
>
> And love one another.
>
> It's all that easy.
>
> And it's all that hard.
>
> Now may the grace of Christ,
>
> The love of God,
>
> And the power of the Holy Spirit.
>
> Be with us all, now and forevermore,
>
> And all God's people say, AMEN.

As of the printing of this book, you can find it online here: www.reyes-chow.com/my-charge-and-benediction/. Please feel free to use it with attribution.

Acknowledgments

Where to begin? Would I get in trouble if I lead off with my dog, Vespa? Too late. My sweet, weirdo, gravel-eating English bull terrier and writing companion, Vespa, died peacefully curled up under her blanket in August 2025. I miss her presence greatly and probably watch too many EBT (English bull terrier) rescue reels on Instagram.

Okay, on to the people.

As always, much love to my family. First to my spouse, Robin, who has to deal with the emotional rhythms, ebbs, and flows of an author who is an Enneagram 3w4. I am sure I am exhausting. Love you. This is also my first book written where all of the children are living on their own. Our not-often-enough family gatherings are always a reminder of how much love and joy have been poured into our collective lives by the ancestors. They are also just funny. Thank you Annie, Abby, and Ev.

For the individuals and groups too numerous to name who have had a hand in developing my understanding of Jesus, especially my collegial group that has been meeting for over twenty-five years—once called the "Young Urban Pastors," now the "Once Were Young Urban Pastors." Thank you, friends, for holding me accountable, being there in times of struggle, and giving me room to be me.

And a big thank-you to the congregations that have shaped my personal faith and pastoral leadership, especially my home church, Trinity Presbyterian Church, Stockton; and the California churches that helped me to grow as a pastor and human: Ocean Avenue Presbyterian Church, San Francisco; Covenant Presbyterian Church, San Francisco; Mission Bay Community Church, San Francisco; Valley Presbyterian Church, Portola Valley; Broadmoor Presbyterian Church, Daly City; First Presbyterian Church, Palo Alto; Filipino Community

United Presbyterian Church, Azusa; Stone Church of Willow Glen, San Jose; Burlington Presbyterian Church, Burlingame, California; and Pasadena Presbyterian Church, Pasadena.

A Word about AI

Between the time I originally signed the contract to write this book and now, the debates about and use of generative AI have exploded. Emotions are running high, opinions are plentiful, and there are no simple answers to the big picture questions about the future or current use of generative AI. For years, we have all been using some form of AI without even realizing it: accessibility tools, spell check, autocorrect, navigation, grammar check, etc., so none of us is pure.

Sadly, the future of writing is going to require some kind of AI disclosures, so, always trying to be ahead of the curve, here are mine:

- Google spell check was used to offer spelling correction suggestions.
- Grammarly was used to offer clarity suggestions, but never for content.
- Otter.ai was used for dictation and voice-to-text, but never to generate content.
- No question was ever asked of ChatGPT, Claude, Gemini, or any other AI platforms to help in the formation or content building of any phase of the writing of this book.

The idea that "the future is now" has never felt so true.

Stay in Touch

Email: bruce@reyes-chow.com

More info about me as well as my newsletter and podcast, *The Amalgamation,* can be found and subscribed to at www.reyes-chow.com.

Social media platforms:

- Bluesky (bit.ly/BRConBS)
- Instagram (bit.ly/BRConIG)
- Facebook (bit.ly/BRConFB)
- TikTok (bit.ly/BRConTT)
- YouTube (bit.ly/BRConYT)
- Threads (bit.ly/BRConTH)
- Mastodon (bit.ly/BRConMA)
- LinkedIn (bit.ly/BRConLI)
- Discord (bit.ly/BRConDC)
- X (bit.ly/BRConX)

Standing Book Group Zoom Offer: If your book group uses this or any of my previous books, if I am able, I would love to join your group via video call for a discussion (for free). To arrange book group meetings and for all other speaking inquiries, please reach out to theteam@reyes-chow.com.

www.ingramcontent.com/pod-product-compliance
Lightning Source LLC
LaVergne TN
LVHW051632200826
845803LV00007B/15